THE HOCHMAN ENCYCLOPEDIA OF AMERICAN PLAYING CARDS
SUPPLEMENT & PRICE GUIDE

Second Edition

COMPANION TO

The Hochman Encyclopedia of American Playing Cards

by Tom and Judy Dawson

U.S. GAMES SYSTEMS, INC.
Publishers
Stamford, CT 06902 USA
www.usgamesinc.com

Tom and Judy Dawson are ardent collectors of antique and unusual playing cards. Their interest in this fast-growing field of collectibles began almost 30 years ago. It grew out of a general enthusiasm for all things antique and their strong penchant for playing card games, especially competitive bridge. In their early collecting days, the Dawsons were fortunate to meet a number of avid collectors, including Gene Hochman, whose enthusiasm and knowledge of early American cards was passed on to them.

The focus of the Dawson's extensive collection is early standard American and Canadian playing cards, as well as the plethora of ephemera related to the cards and their makers.

Before retirement Tom enjoyed a long and successful career as a senior partner in Deloitte & Touche. He presently holds a number of corporate directorships and pursues other interests including family, duplicate bridge, and golf. Judy raised their six children and continues to enjoy gardening, home design, and other areas of antique collecting.

In addition to caring for their growing card collection, Tom and Judy find time to serve as officers of "52 Plus Joker," a club for those interested in antique American playing cards. Judy also edits the club's quarterly publication, *Clear the Decks*.

THE HOCHMAN ENCYCLOPEDIA OF AMERICAN PLAYING CARDS SUPPLEMENT & PRICE GUIDE SECOND EDITION

ISBN 1-57281-310-5 • Item # APC60

Published by
U.S. GAMES SYSTEMS, INC.
179 Ludlow Street
Stamford, CT 06902 USA
www.usgamesinc.com

©2004 U.S. GAMES SYSTEMS, INC.

THE HOCHMAN ENCYCLOPEDIA OF AMERICAN PLAYING CARDS

Supplement & Price Guide

IN OCTOBER 2000 THE HOCHMAN ENCYCLOPEDIA of American Playing Cards was published, along with a complementary Price Guide, as an aid to collectors, researchers and all individuals with an interest in old or unusual American playing cards. The Encyclopedia was a consolidation of a set of six volumes originally produced by Gene Hochman from 1976 to 1981, with a significant amount of new information and listings added to update the work.

Three years have passed since the Encyclopedia was published, and additional information, based on new research and new discoveries, has been accumulated, much of it from fellow collectors. During this period, the marketplace has influenced the prices of old playing cards, in many cases quite significantly.

We therefore decided to publish this Supplement & Price Guide to share the information we discovered. The revisions, with pictures where possible, are included in the first section. In addition, errors in the original book have been corrected and new information and listings have been added.

The second section is a complete revision of the Price Guide, reflecting transactions observed over the past several years, in an effort to provide updated prices for the use of all those trading in old and unusual American playing cards.

The material in this edition is presented in the same order as the material in the original Encyclopedia—new information and discoveries are listed under chapter numbers and headings.

We would like to thank all those who have contributed to this supplement. Many of those who helped previously have sent us additional information. In addition several new contributors including Pauline & Skip Young, Graham & Kay Curtis, Larry Laevens, Anthony Sammarco, and Chris Hinchcliffe have forwarded us information and/or material on new finds.

Tom and Judy Dawson

ENCYCLOPEDIA CHAPTER 2
Collecting Playing Cards

Correction: Page 5—In the paragraphs on value in the Price Guide the term "Very Good" is used as the third pricing category. There was an inconsistency between this and the term "Good" used in the paragraphs on value on page 5. We believe "Very Good" is the correct terminology.

ENCYCLOPEDIA CHAPTER 3
Early Makers

Correction: Page 10—The reference for Henry Hart of New York in the table should be "U39."

Note: Page 12—Information from a newspaper article entitled The Devil's Pictures from the Boston Globe of April 30, 1905 sheds additional light on Thomas Crehore and his playing card manufactory. Crehore was born in 1769 in Dorchester, just outside Boston, a fifth generation descendant of Teague Crehore. He commenced the manufacture of playing cards in 1798, and, in 1801, he purchased for $2,800 the land and two houses he needed for the expansion of his already successful business. Crehore became a successful investor in local real estate and in 1831 took up residence in Boston. One can surmise that his sons were by then actively engaged in the business. As a final note, it is interesting that Crehore was a significant factor in the reduction of duties on the importation of playing cards during the period of his manufacturing—perhaps he was also an importer of British cards.

New: U3a THOMAS CREHORE

Dorchester, Mass., c1825. This deck was reputedly made by Crehore and we estimate it to be in the 1820–1830 period. The Heart King is virtually identical to the one from U3.

U3a king *U3a ace*

Note: Page 13—As further evidence that Hart manufactured the 'Bartlet' cards, the pictured wrapper, found with a hart deck, has a 1 cent revenue stamp with the initials 'CB' and a cancellation date of Dec. 1862.

Hart wrapper

Note: Page 14—The pictured wrapper with the title "Fisk's Eagle Cards" and the initials W.T.F. was found recently. It contained a deck of Caleb Bartlett cards with the U7 Ace of Spades.

U7 wrapper

Note: Page 18—Additional information from Michael Goodall confirms that Victor Mauger manufactured Goodall cards for sale in the United States as well as the brands he marketed under his own name. One of these brands, in addition to those mentioned in the paragraph following the description of U19c, was Tugboats.

New Listing: U34a E PLURIBUS UNUM

Unknown manufacture, c1840. This Ace is identical to the Emporium Ace of U34, except for the omission of the initials "J. & L. D." and the word "Emporium." Most logically it was made by the same manufacturer. The courts are significantly different, being rich in color with flesh tones and appearing more regal.

U34a ace *U34a king*

ENCYCLOPEDIA CHAPTER 4
Longley Brothers
and Successor Companies

Note: L13 CENTENNIAL PLAYING CARDS

Longley & Bro., Cincinnati, 1876. A number of cards from another deck of these Centennial cards surfaced quite recently. It is interesting that they have a different back than those in the USPC Playing Card Museum, because one would expect that all the example decks printed would have the same back design. Is it possible a few decks were issued after all?

L13 back

New Listing:
L14a AMERICAN CLUB #165

Paper Fabrique Company, Cincinnati, c1878. The picture shows a similar Ace of Spades with an eagle in the center of the pip in place of the hand with a spread of cards.

L14a ace

Correction: Page 28—The reference in the description of L21 to L78 should be L79.

Note: Page 29—Another deck linking Chicago Card Co. to Crescent Card Co. has the L24 Ace, L25 courts and L25b Joker. The back advertises their playing cards as "the best and cheapest."

New Listing: L25c HAWLEY

Hawley Card Co., Chicago, c1895. This deck, from an unknown maker, has a Joker that strongly resembles the Novelty Joker of L28b, and comes with the same courts as L25a.

L25c ace   *L25c joker*

Note: Page 30—Another deck, named Charter Oak # 1899 on the box, has been found with the L26 Ace of Spades and L25 courts.

Note: L41 UNION PCC

New York, c1885. An example of this Union PCC deck with a special Lillian Russell back. Unfortunately it was found without a box or Joker.

L41 back

Note: L43 UNION PCC

Two other brands with the L43 Ace of Spades are Stag and Travelers. Both were found with the Joker pictured in the middle of the listing.

Note: L56 PREMIERS

The Premiers Joker pictured as L56 also comes in a version with no writing.

Note: Page 43—An example of a brand mentioned in the original book as Imperials #25 (#35) has been found with the L55 Ace of Spades and Joker.

Note:
L57a GOLFETTE #53

APCC, c1900. The Joker for this whist-size deck is similar to the Golf Joker of L57.

L57a joker

Note:
L63 DERBY #30 (#330)

APCC, c1895. Another Joker for this scarce brand has been discovered.

L63 joker

Note:
L66 SPANISH PLAYING CARDS

APPC, c1895. The picture in the original book was of poor quality. Pictured here are the 4 of Cups, 4 of Coins and 12 (King) of Swords.

L66 King

L66 4 of Coins   *L66 4 of Cups*

New Listing: L71a APCC

APCC, c1895. Another Joker with a standard APCC Ace of Spades. The Joker is remarkably similar to SU23. Until the brand name is discovered we will classify it as L71a.

L71a joker

New image: L82 COLUMBIA PCC

c1890. The back mentioned in the original Encyclopedia is shown in this picture. Columbia decks have been discovered that have backs normally used by APCC, adding credence to the theory that it is part of the Longley group.

L82 back

ENCYCLOPEDIA CHAPTER 5
New York Consolidated Card Company

Note: Page 46—We have included a scan of an L.I. Cohen price list. Though undated, it is likely from the early 1860s.

L.I. Cohen pricelist

New: NY6a ILLUMINATED

New York, c1845. This deck has the same courts as the L. I. Cohen illuminated deck NY6. Was the deck made by them for export, or was it an attempt to indicate it was "imported?" In any event, we are confident this deck was produced by Cohen on his four-color press.

NY6a ace

New image: NY8 LAWRENCE, COHEN & CO.

1863. This great "Civil War" version of this listing comes with a patriotic back and matching wrapper, printed in bright red, white and blue.

NY8 back   *NY8 wrapper*

Note: NY10 LAWRENCE & COHEN & CO.

c1863. This deck also comes in a handsome slipcase, decorated with portions of its original wrapper, with the word "Eagles" at one end.

Note: NY15 John J. Levy—Portions of the wrapper for the NY15 deck indicate it was called "Gallant Highlanders."

Correction: Page 50—The "wrapper" shown is actually the NY10 Ace of Spades.

New: NY20a UNION CARD MANUFACTORY

New York, c1855. This deck has the same courts as NY19 but a quite different Ace of Spades, somewhat akin to NY17.

NY20a ace

Note: Page 53—Henry Cohen was known to be in the same type of stationery business as L. I. Cohen in 1845 in Philadelphia. His establishment was at 3 S. 4th Street and L. I. Cohen & Co. was at 27 S. 4th Street! Note that 27 S. 4th Street was also used by Samuel Hart when he started in business about that time. Likely the NY27b deck by Henry Cohen was made in the 1840s and not in the 1860s as originally thought.

New: NY31b JONES & CO.

Philadelphia, c1860. When we saw this Ace of Spades we assumed it was one of the first English illuminated decks. Subsequent investigation determined that Jones & Co. was a name used by Charles Bartlett to pass off locally made decks as "imported." No doubt Hart decided to trade on the Jones & Co. name as well, as his manufactory had, to some extent, commenced with machinery and plates from Bartlett. What confirmed our suspicion that it was made by Hart, was the comparison of the courts to colored photos we had of the beautiful Hart Illuminated NY31a, showing them to be identical. This Ace is quite colorful—featuring red flowers and pip center, green foliage, and touches of blue. The crown, pip outline, etc. are illuminated in gold.

NY31b ace

New: NY36b LONDON CLUB CARD

Samuel Hart & Co., Philadelphia & New York, c1865. This Ace clearly falls in between NY36 and NY36a. It has the same Joker as NY36.

NY36b ace

Note: Page 57—An interesting Best Bower Joker, virtually identical to NY46 but remaining unnamed, was found as part of a deck made in the 1890s by Grimaud of France!

Note: Page 58—Early Squeezer #35 brands included #35 First Squeezers, Gem Whist, Mascotte and Montana Rough Riders.

New: NY50d SQUEEZERS #35

c1898. A new Ace found on a deck made for export to Argentina.

NY50d ace

Note: NY60 BEE #92—A Bee deck has been found with a Best Bower Joker similar to NY47a. Presumably this was the first Joker used by Bee before it established its own proprietary Joker.

Note: Page 66—The Franco-American #112 deck without indices is named "non-squeezers" on the box.

ENCYCLOPEDIA CHAPTER 6
Andrew Dougherty

Note: Page 73—The AD17a deck is known to come with the clown Joker from AD12.

Note: Page 77—Other named Marguerite cards found in a sample book recently are Sweet Sixteen, Vanity, Lilacs, and Violets. Rather than flowers, Lilacs and Violets card backs feature pictures of women carrying small bouquets.

ENCYCLOPEDIA CHAPTER 7
The United States
Playing Card Company

Note: Page 85—Army & Navy #303, US5d also comes with the US5a Joker.

Note: Page 86—The lacquer back decks came with both #606 and #404 and were sometimes outlined in other metallic style colors such as green and bronze. The Dundreary Joker pictured in the book within the oval frame also came without "US" in the corners.

Note: Page 87—US6cc comes with the second Dundreary Joker of US6.

Note: Page 88—Multi #666 Congress was manufactured in two finishes, either air-cushioned or enameled.

Note: Page 90—The high wheel Joker of US8 is known to have come with US8a as well.

New: *US8fa* BICYCLE BRIDGE #86

USPC–RM Fact., c1922. The pictured Joker for this deck will appeal to golfers. It is printed in multiple colors.

US8fa joker

Note: Page 94—Correspondence between a jobber in Nebraska and a customer stated that "Texan #45 are made to correspond with Harts Cards #319. They are better and tougher stock than either 155 or 808 (Editor's note—Tourist #155 and Bicycle #808), but the finish is different. They are made more especially for gamblers and are a very hard finished card without enamel."

Correction: Page 96—The comment under US18 that the deck is pictured below as US18-2 is erroneous, the latter being a US Printing Co. Ace.

Correction: *US38* FAUNTLEROY #29

The US38 description should indicate R&M, not RMP.

Correction: Page 104—The pictures listed as US39 are actually for both versions of Little Duke #24.

Note: Page 105—Hornet #6, US46, also came with a generic Joker similar to US47.

Correction: Page 106—Tower Mfg., US53, is likely dated about 1925, not 1905.

New: *US60* SCOUT #108

USPC, 1910. This newly discovered brand was advertised in England in 1910. The pictured box is from the ad.

US60 box

ENCYCLOPEDIA CHAPTER 8
The National Card Company

Note: Page 109—An element of confusion exists about the early days of National Card Company and the role of Samuel J. Murray. The Encyclopedia states he left Russell & Morgan in 1886 to establish NCC and came back to United States Printing Co. when they bought National in 1893. We now know that he was the R&M foreman in 1889, according to a contemporary article about Russell & Morgan. In addition the original listings showed estimated dates for the early National brands as prior to 1886. Speculation would be that he actually left R&M earlier and had returned by 1889, perhaps leaving someone else in charge of National in Indianapolis. Hopefully one day this mystery will be cleared up.

New images: *NU6c* ALADDIN #1004

(USPC), 1928. This deck was not pictured in the original work.

NU6c cards

Note: *NU14* TENNIS #144

APCC, c1890. A Joker found with a Tennis #144, NU14 deck, is remarkably similar, yet quite different, to the usual Joker with the Brownie deck, L76. We have shown them both here for comparison. The new find appears to be the brownies at play in the snow "before" while the Brownies #35 shows them "after" some of them have been bombed by the giant snowballs.

NU14 joker   *L76 joker*

ENCYCLOPEDIA CHAPTER 9
Perfection Playing Card Company

Note: Page 118—Decks with the PU4 Ace of Spades have been discovered with the Joker from PU3. In addition the Joker pictured is from another PU4 deck. The Joker has a red hat, a red splotchy face and a decidedly red nose! Finally we have another PU4 deck that comes in a "Bunker Hill Playing Cards—Bankers #260" box.

PU4 joker

CHAPTER 10
Pyramid Playing Card Company

New listing: *PY8b GOLF*

Brooklyn, c1924. The Joker from another Pyramid deck with the PY8 Ace (except there is no brand name on the Ace) entitled Golf.

PY8b joker

Note: Page 123—The back of the Kismet deck, PY10, has a portrait of Conrad J. Dykeman, Potentate of the Temple in 1906–07 and Imperial Potentate in 1923. The Joker for this deck pictures the temple on Herkimer St. in Brooklyn.

ENCYCLOPEDIA CHAPTER 11
Russell

Note: Page 126—Russell's Regulars, RU5, also came in a slipcase marked "Russell's Ideal Playing Cards, Gilt-edged, Seconds".

ENCYCLOPEDIA CHAPTER 12
Standard Playing Card Manufacturing Company

New listing: *SU1a MONITOR BRAND STEAMBOATS*

Standard Playing Card Co., Chicago, c1890. Another brand utilizing the SU1 Ace of Spades. The courts are most unusual and unlike other Standard decks.

SU1a joker   *SU1a king*

New listing: *SU13a AUSTEN BEAUTIES #506*

Chicago, c1895. This variation does not mention Austen Beauties on the Ace but does so on the variation of the normal Standard Joker used. Like all SU13 listings, it has a portrait of a "Beauty" on the card back.

SU13a cards

New listing: *SU14a BUFFET*

Chicago, c1895. A variation of SU14 with "(BUFFET)" printed on the Ace. The colored Joker is quite unusual.

SU14a ace   *SU14a joker*

ENCYCLOPEDIA CHAPTER 13
Other Makers

New listing: MSW144 STAR

Boston c1895. This could be a brand made by NYCC for a stationer or store. The Ace is unusual but the back and court cards suggest NYCC.

MSW144 ace   MSW144 back

ENCYCLOPEDIA CHAPTER 14
Narrow Cards

Note: MSN4a ENARDOE

The Enardoe cards made by E. O. Drane in 1932 also came in a regular version—black spades, etc.

New listing: MSN6b ARRCO

Chicago, c1940. Two more Arrco Aces

MSN6b ace   MSN6b ace 2

Note: Page 155—The Permanite deck by Cruver, MSN31, could also be classified as a non-revoke deck because of the use of a suit sign within the pip and as an oddities because of the permanent plastic material used in its manufacture. Similarly, MSN32 could be classified in oddities.

Correction: MSN71 HALLMARK

Recent information dates the first Hallmark cards as 1961, not 1940. Their first cards were made in Germany, with later cards being produced by Arrco. The deck pictured as MSN71 was likely produced about 1970.

New: MSN71a HALLMARK

c1961. This is one of the early decks made in West Germany for Hallmark. Note they were of a larger size.

MSN71a ace   MSN71a joker

New: MSN74a WESTERN

c1935. Another Western PCC deck with two Jokers used with this Ace.

MSN74a ace   MSN74a joker   MSN74a joker

New listing: MSN80 CHARME

c1935. This brand was likely manufactured by USPC.

MSN80 ace   MSN80 joker

ENCYCLOPEDIA CHAPTER 16
Canadian Standard Playing Cards

Note: Page 170—The Ace of Spades shown as CDN5b, together with the Joker of CDN5a, were used for other brands including Oak Leaf, Owl and Good Luck #280.

Note: Page 171—Decks with the CDN9 Ace also have been found in patience size.

New listing: *CDN24b USPC*

c1935. This Ace and Joker were found on a deck advertising British Consul Cigarettes.

CDN24b ace   *CDN24b joker*

Note: Page 174—We stated that all wide Congress #606 decks sold in Canada were made in Cincinnati. We have since discovered a Congress #606 deck, Beacon Light, with a Toronto Ace of Spades.

Note: *CDN26 APOLLO #33*

c1921. In the Encyclopedia we speculated that the Ace and Joker for this brand was similar to its U.S. counterpart. Subsequently we found this deck with a very similar Ace and identical Joker. The Ace says The U.S. Playing Card Co. in the place of The National Card Co. and the banner at the bottom reads Windsor Ont. Canada. The box says Toronto, indicating manufacture just after the move to Windsor. No doubt versions produced a few years earlier in Toronto would have looked almost the same.

CDN26 ace   *CDN26 joker*

New: *CDN33a CHAS. J. MITCHELL*

Toronto, c1890. A version of this deck, produced as insert cards, was discovered last year. We have pictured the Ace and the Queen of Clubs here and it is cross-referenced to a new listing ICA11.

CDN33a ace   *CDN33a court*

New: *CDN36a THE PEARSALL CARD CO.*

c1890. A version with indices. We can assume the Joker in CDN36 was the same.

CDN36a ace   *CDN36a joker*

New listing: *CDN41 BEAUCHEMIN & VALOIS*

c1885. Beauchemin & Valois were book publishers in Montreal in the late 1800s. We suspect this square cornered deck—with the very Canadian beaver and maple leaf, but very U.S. spade pip with stars and stripes—was made in Belgium for this company.

CDN41 ace   *CDN41 king*

New: *CDN42 CANADIAN CARD CO.*

c1885. Another Canadian old square cornered deck. We are more certain than ever that this deck was manufactured in Belgium.

CDN42 ace *CDN42 king*

ENCYCLOPEDIA CHAPTER 17
Advertising Playing Cards

New Image: *AA1 DR. RANSOM'S*

c1875. The picture of the Spade Five in the Encyclopedia was not clear so we have reproduced it here along with the Ace of Spades and Joker.

AA1 ace *AA1 joker*

AA1 five

ENCYCLOPEDIA CHAPTER 19
Insert Cards

Note: Page 211—Another Deep Run Hunt Club Whiskey deck has been found—this one advertises Saunders & Chambers, not E. A. Saunders Sons.

New: *I13 HARD A PORT*

c1890. The coupon pictured explains that by remitting 48 coupons one could obtain a briar pipe or "a beautiful pack of Hard A Port Playing Cards."

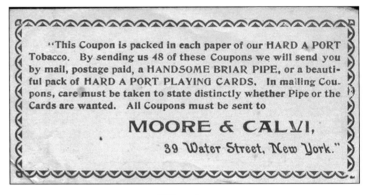

I13 coupon

New: *ICA11 CHAS. J. MITCHELL*

Toronto, c1890. This newly discovered Canadian insert deck is patterned after the regular Mitchell deck listed as CDN33 and also listed in that chapter as CDN33a.

ICA11 ace *ICA11 three*

ICA11 back

New: W24 FREEDOM PLAYING CARDS

Portland, 1917. Another "No Kings or Queens for Me" Joker showing the royal crowns being swept away.

W24 joker

New: W51 CENTENNIAL PLAYING CARDS

Cincinnati, 1876. This deck, commemorating the Revolutionary War of 1776, should also have been listed in this chapter (refer L13).

ENCYCLOPEDIA CHAPTER 21
Political and Patriotic Cards

New image: P15a VOTES FOR WOMEN II

APCC, c1910. The Joker for this deck.

P15a joker   *P15b back*

New: P15b VOTES FOR WOMEN

Western PCC, c1915. Another Votes for Women deck, this time wide, with a regular Western Ace and Joker.

New: P15c VOTES FOR WOMEN

1975. A more recent deck of "Ms. Playing Cards" with the remembrance of the suffragette movement on the card back.

P15c ace   *P15c back*

New: P24 RUSSIAN MONARCH PLAYING CARDS

Roxbury, Mass., 1909. A fascinating deck published by J. Dravin that focuses on the period of Russian history surrounding the revolution in 1905. Each suit has its own color scheme, clubs: yellow, hearts: green, diamonds: red, and spades: mauve. The Spade Ace indicates the dooming of the first constitutional effort and the King of that suit, Pyotr Stolypin, was, in part, responsible for its fate. The Heart King is Count Sergei Witte, tutor to the Grand Duke Michael. The Joker features the dancing Clown-Tsar. Further details about this deck are in an article published in the IPCS Playing Card in March–April 2002.

P24 ace

P24 joker   *P24 king*

New: P25 SOCKEM WITH TAXES

Capitol Card Co., 1936. This deck has four suits—Farmer, Labor, Capital, and Taxes. The additional 14th card in the suit of Taxes was called Brain Trust Tax, and could be used as a Joker. It was designed on behalf of the Republican Party for use in the 1936 election, where they were soundly defeated as President Roosevelt won his second term. Pictured here are the "King" of Farmers, the "Joker" and the back with the Republican elephant.

P25c king

P25c joker   *P25c back*

ENCYCLOPEDIA CHAPTER 22
Entertainment

New images: SE16 BASEBALL BACKS

1906. In all there are six of the Willis Russell baseball backs. They are pictured here along with a 1910 schedule produced on the back of one of these cards.

SE16 backs (above)

SE16 extra card   *SE16 box*

New: SE38 BATTER UP

1908. This baseball game has been overprinted on a Dougherty Steamboat deck with gold edges. Shown are the the Spade Ace one game card and the box. The twos all say "FOUL", the nines feature baseball terms, and ten of the cards have stars.

SE38 ace   *SE38 two*   *SE38 box*

ENCYCLOPEDIA CHAPTER 23
Fortune Telling

Correction: Page 242—The correct name is Petrtyl. The Green Spade Tarot deck has 78 cards; Tarcock version has 54 cards.

Note: Page 244—Nile Fortune Telling, FT11, also comes with the fortunes inverted on the Spade Ace and no fortunes on the courts.

New: FT25 SABINA

1908. Another fortune telling deck which comes with advertising on the backs for John Miles Wholesale Millinery Goods in New York.

FT25 card   *FT25 box*

FT25 back

ENCYCLOPEDIA CHAPTER 24
Exposition and World's Fair

New: SX19a ALUMINUM PLAYING CARDS

1901. The same deck as SX19 but with a special back for the Fifth Annual Masquerade of the Calumet Club in Racine, Wis. The Joker is also pictured. The deck, in its aluminum case, came inside a special red cardboard box.

SX19a joker   *SX19a back*

ENCYCLOPEDIA CHAPTER 25
Wide Souvenirs

New: *S37a NEW YORK CITY SOUVENIR PLAYING CARDS*

c1915. This deck has Type D photos and appears to have been made by the Advertising Card Co.

S37A back

New images: *S78 MACATAWA BAY SOUVENIR CARDS*

c1890. In the original Encyclopedia we mentioned that we did not know anyone who had actually seen this deck. Well, one has finally turned up and we show a few cards here.

S78 back *S78 joker*

S78 king *S78 ten*

Note: Page 263—S85 Lancaster Souvenir Playing Cards also comes with a back advertising "Conestoga Photo Engraving Co."

ENCYCLOPEDIA CHAPTER 27
Canadian and Other Souvenirs

New: *SO4 PERU SOUVENIR PLAYING CARDS*

c1905. This deck has Type A photos and appears to have been made by USPC.

SO4 back

Note: Page 272—We also understand that there are several more souvenir decks made in the United States in the early 20th century for South America, including a third Peruvian deck and two decks for Brazil.

ENCYCLOPEDIA CHAPTER 29
Bridge and Whist

Note: Page 283—BW34 Whist Cards for Practice comes with the regular Capitol Joker.

ENCYCLOPEDIA CHAPTER 31
New Suits

New: *NS27 PAHLAVI*

1903. This deck, designed for "Instruction Games and Cartomancy" has new suit signs and comes with two "Jokers."

 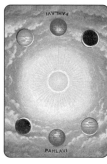 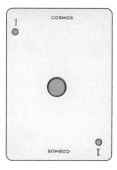

NS27 ace *NS27 back* *NS27 ace 2*

CHAPTER 32
Novelties

Note: Page 300—Globe Playing Cards, O28, came in a similar version with the address 50 Bromfield St. Boston. It likely dates between O28 and O15, Waterproof Playing Cards.

MEYER BROTHERS DRUGGISTS   (Supplement)

Front of American Playing Cards Price List, circa 1895

THIS SUPPLEMENT & PRICE GUIDE complements *The Hochman Encyclopedia of American Playing Cards*, published in October 2000. Readers familiar with the Price Guide issued in 2000 will note that there are many changes. These reflect transactions in the marketplace that we, and other experts we consulted, have observed over the last three years. Transactions reviewed include playing card sales through collectors' auctions and fixed price lists, antique paper and ephemera shows, and internet sales—especially through the eBay auction site.

It is important to remark at the outset that this Price Guide is only a guide. It is not a price list, and buyers will often find that a price being asked differs from the amount indicated in this Guide. However, our goal is to help both buyers and sellers of old American playing cards establish a fair starting point for transactions.

The order of the listings here follows *The Hochman Encyclopedia of American Playing Cards*. Standard cards are listed first, followed by those with a significant crossover interest, fortune telling and tarot cards, souvenir decks, and finally, oddities, novelties and non-standard decks used for Whist and Bridge. A few comments about specific categories follow:

STANDARD DECKS

The prices of standard decks are more difficult to estimate than those established for popular categories such as transformation and insert cards, souvenir and railway cards and advertising decks. Non-standard decks usually have beautiful and/or interesting courts, can be of historical significance, and often appeal to more than one group of collectors. Accordingly, the law of supply and demand makes standard cards generally less expensive. Many of the decks listed in this book in Chapters 3 to 16 are rarer (several are likely unique) than decks selling for much higher prices in other categories. Novelty, souvenir, political, transformation, and other non-standard decks were often preserved and placed in a hidden nook to be found and collected many years later. This was not usually the case with standard decks. Invariably they were bought to be played with, and were almost always discarded when soiled or worn.

Many brands used a variety of jokers during their existence. Some of these are very rare and have a much higher appeal to collectors and therefore add extra value to the deck in question. Instances of this phenomenon can be found in many chapters. For example RU18 or SU4 values can range from $15 to $400 or more depending on which of the pictured jokers comes with the deck.

In a similar fashion, the back used on a standard deck can have greater or lesser appeal, thus affecting value. For example, a simple pattern back on AD7 is less desirable than the scarce back sometimes used with the maker's initials entwined into the elaborate design. Similarly, Treasury #89 (US18a) floral back decks command a significantly higher price than those with the less exciting, patterned backs. Finally, decks such as Congress #606, that were made with backs designed to appeal to the consumers of the day, have varying values depending on their current appeal to collectors and their relative rarity.

Only ardent collectors seem to have any interest in the varieties of standard decks, a mistake, in our opinion, as they are the backbone of the history of playing cards. This impacts the pricing of standard decks. For example, a rare 19th century standard deck may be priced less than a 19th century war deck—though there may be many more copies of the war deck in the marketplace.

DECKS WITH CROSSOVER INTEREST

Many playing cards have an interest to collectors in other fields. For playing card collectors, this is a two-edged sword. The desire of collectors in other fields to obtain a certain deck that fits into their special area of interest can have a significant impact on the demand, and therefore the price, of the deck. We have all experienced the surprise of seeing a deck we thought might be worth $100, sell for many times that because of this crossover interest. This is fine when we are selling, but disconcerting when we are competing to buy.

Advertising decks in particular can have a broad range of appeal. We have learned that when competing for Coca-Cola or Maxfield Parrish decks, we have to pay significantly more than if the cards advertised a less desirable product or were designed by a less popular artist. A dramatic example would be the earliest Coke advertising deck in excellent condition that might command a price of $12,000, whereas an equally scarce deck advertising a relatively unknown drink of the same era might only be worth $300. We have therefore used averages in the Price Guide for decks in the "AB," "AC," and "AD" categories—because decks advertising specific products and decks with unusual features can often demand a significant premium.

The same principle, although less pronounced, applies to other areas of collecting. For example, crossover interests can have a material effect on the value of early sports playing cards, particularly baseball. In addition, political, war, entertainment, tobacco insert, transformation, railway, and souvenir decks are often of strong interest to other collectors, with the resultant impact on their value.

WIDE SOUVENIR DECKS

Wide souvenir decks with different scenes on the face of each card were plentiful in the period from about 1890 to the mid-1920s. Many of these decks are still around today and they are often in mint or excellent condition. This is primarily because, as souvenirs of an event or place, they were taken home, put away, and never played with. This contradictory aspect of souvenir playing cards was compounded by the fact that they were difficult to play with—the scenes made it much harder to determine the suit and rank of each card when a number of cards were held in one's hand.

It is often surprising to a dealer or a non-collector of playing cards that a mint example of an interesting and beautiful deck with 53 different views that dates back to the early 1900s, might only be worth $50. Of course, supply and demand is the determinant and the fact that these decks were often produced in large quantities means there is a large supply of mint and excellent copies of many of these souvenir decks.

Having said that, there are a number of souvenir type decks that are truly scarce and a number that also appeal to collectors in other fields. The Burro deck (S10) is an example of the former and the American Indian Blanket Back deck (S3) an example of the latter, being of strong interest to collectors of early North American Indian artifacts, pictures, etc. Again, the laws of supply and demand prevail, and the rare Burro deck commands a price close to $1,200. The relatively common American Indian deck, usually sells in a range from $300 to $500 for a mint example. (There are exceptions—an American Indian deck sold for as much as $1,400 in a specialty auction.)

Because almost all of these decks are known and catalogued, there are a number of people who are attempting to obtain a copy of each of the listed decks, and several whose collections in this field are almost complete. While it is relatively easy for these collectors to eventually obtain an example of most of the decks, they are usually in the market for examples that will upgrade their collection. This is one of the reasons why, except for the most common decks, "as issued" and "mint" examples command a substantial premium.

We have tried to take into account condition, scarcit,y and the interests of other collectors in establishing prices for souvenir and scenic railway decks. In addition, collectors specializing in this area have reviewed our determinations and their suggestions have been incorporated. The resultant prices are indicative of the current marketplace.

OTHER NON-STANDARD DECKS

The remaining categories of non-standard decks cover a wide range of topics, and while of interest to some, generally do not appeal to a wide number of collectors. For this reason, they usually can be obtained for a reasonable price and can be a good place for beginning collectors to start. Again, most of the decks in these categories have been discovered and cataloged, and the collector can attempt to obtain an example of each listing in a particular category, for example, no-revoke decks or decks with new suit signs.

CONDITION

We have repeated below some of the information contained in Chapter 1 of the Encyclopedia. This includes comments on condition, a very important aspect of value. In fact, we believe that the impact of condition on value has become more pronounced during the years we have been collecting. Decks that are almost in the same condition as when they left the factory, appear to command a larger premium than previously. Collectors seem to be more discerning, and desire near mint examples of their favorite decks for their collections.

Like any collectible, the condition of playing cards has an important role in desirability and thus in their value. We would all like our decks to be sparkling mint and still in their original wrappers and/or boxes. Unfortunately, most decks that collectors find have seen at least moderate use and thus have probably lost some element of their desirability.

Nonetheless, most collectors will happily buy a less than perfect example to fill a hole in their collection, with the hope of upgrading their purchase in the future.

While terminology relative to assessing the condition of playing cards has not been standardized, most collectors would agree that "as issued" means the deck is close to the same condition as when it left the factory. The deck may have been opened but not removed from its package, and certainly it should never have been played with. If even the slightest element, e.g. a cellophane wrapper, is missing from an otherwise pristine deck, it could not be classified as "as issued"—rather it would be "mint." If the missing element is of more consequence it would likely be further downgraded.

Gene Hochman devised the following system to describe decks of playing cards:

"As issued"—a complete deck, in mint condition, including all cards, jokers and extra cards contained in the original packaging when first distributed for sale. It may be unopened or carefully opened for examination, but not played with. If applicable, the tax stamp, broken or not, should be attached.

"Mint"—a complete deck showing no signs of use. Normally all cards should be present as well as the original box in mint or near mint condition. The inside wrapper need not be included.

"Excellent"—a complete deck that has been occasionally used, but still in first class condition. Gold edges should still be intact and you would be proud to use this deck in your game.

"Good"–A complete deck showing signs of repeated use, but still in useable condition. There should be no serious creases or bent/broken corners. The deck should not be swollen or misshapen and it must fit comfortably into the original box.

"Poor"—A deck not good enough to fit into one of the above categories. It likely would have at least one of these serious faults—bent or broken corners, bad creases, heavy soiling, etc.

"With Faults"—A deck in one of the "Good" to "As issued" categories, but with a serious fault like a missing or damaged card or a damaged, incomplete, or missing box.

The above descriptions were developed by Gene at the time of writing the original Encyclopedia and have stood the test of time. Many collectors have introduced variations into their cataloging, e.g. "mint plus," "mint," and "mint minus". In addition, it has become popular to describe the condition of a deck's box as OB1 (basically mint), OB2 (some damage but complete) or OB3 (quite heavily damaged and/or some portion missing). Nonetheless, use of the above descriptions and a careful notation of anything that is missing will provide an appropriate listing for cataloging purposes.

In all attempts to describe a deck, it is important to mention everything that is included, plus anything that is missing. For example, a brief description of an early advertising deck might read as follows:

"Advertising deck from 1910 for Dawson's Old Time Ale. Mint condition, in original box (slight damage to flap) with dated 2¢ U.S. revenue stamp. Includes 53 cards with advertising Ace of Spades and special advertising Joker. The extra advertising card is missing and the Club Jack has a small smudge."

A note on completeness: most decks issued in America before the late 1860s were issued with only 52 cards. In the transition period between 1865 and 1880, manufacturers often added a blank card or a Joker. After the mid-1870s most decks came with 52 cards plus a Joker and one additional card—generally a blank, a scoring card card or an advertising card. The main exceptions were certain decks that were manufactured with different European suit signs and styles. Decks made for specific games often came without Jokers and had fewer cards, such as 32-card Euchre, 48-card Pinochle, and 52-card Whist. We should note that in the second half of the 20th century it became quite common for a deck to contain two Jokers.

The extra cards over and above the regular 52 and joker(s) are clearly of less importance—a deck lacking one is hardly devalued. However, the extra cards in wide advertising decks (which usually depict a factory, a separate ad, a price list, etc.) are more important. The pips in an important deck, especially one with unusual or non-standard courts, are of lesser importance than the courts. A missing Ace of Spades or Joker is the most serious deficiency.

Despite most people's desire to collect only "as issued" or "mint" decks, collectors will still rejoice at finding a deck in "good" condition if it is high on their want list or quite scarce. Often it will be purchased with the expectation that the same deck in better condition will someday replace it.

VALUING OLD PLAYING CARDS

We have decided to use only three levels of condition in determining the values in this supplement. They are:

"Mint"—a complete deck showing no signs of use. Normally all cards should be present as should the original box in mint or near mint condition. The inside wrapper would not need to be there.

"Excellent"—a complete deck that has been occasionally used, but is still in first-class condition. Gold edges should still be intact and you would be proud to use this deck in your game.

"Very Good"—A complete deck showing signs of repeated use, but still useable. There should be no serious creases or bent/broken corners. The deck should not be swollen or misshapen and should fit comfortably into the original box.

Prices for decks in the other categories can be interpolated from those shown. For example, a deck that is "as issued" would command a premium, perhaps substantial, over the mint price. This is especially true for decks from the 19th century that still have their wrappers and/or boxes intact and are in excellent condition. Conversely a deck that is in poor condition would be worth less than a "very good" one, and one with faults would likely be subject to a significant discount from the "very good" price.

We have tried to be conservative in our pricing. Many times decks in superb condition will command a significant premium over the listed price. A deck with a scarce Joker can be worth substantially more than the same deck with its normal Joker (e.g. US8 with rare colored Joker).

There are still quite a few decks where the number of known copies can be counted on the fingers of one hand. Many of these are in museum collections and many of the very early decks, listed "mint" may not even exist in that condition, but the category is priced on the basis that one or more may become available in the future.

When using this guide in determining the value of any deck of cards, keep in mind that, while it has been compiled from auction lists and decks offered for sale by antique dealers, internet and other auctions, rare book shops and private collectors, the prices are nonetheless somewhat subjective. As sales of rarer decks are few and far between, a particular collector's desire for a certain deck can often result in an unrealistic price. Or, the sudden entry on the market of a few copies of a scarce deck can result in sales with prices substantially less than previously obtained.

We have tried to take note of decks that appear to be present in most collections as well as those that are scarce and wanted by many different collectors. As discussed earlier, prices must also be based on the number of collecting fields an individual deck might encompass. For example, a baseball deck will appeal to baseball nostalgia collectors as well as playing card collectors. An advertising deck from the Columbian Exposition will be sought by World's Fair and advertising collectors, as well as those in our field. In the final analysis, scarcity of the item, condition and the law of supply and demand will determine the price.

In Hochman's last issued price list in 1991 he presented some advice for both buyers and sellers. It was, and still is good advice, and we repeat it here: *"advice to buyers .... if you see a deck that you really want for your collection and you have an opportunity to buy it, and the price seems higher than the listed value, remember you may never find another .... and if you do, it will probably be for more. Even if you overpay slightly, it will not be long before the value will surpass the purchase price. Advice to sellers .... using this list as "the price" you must get, will result in many lost sales. You must find a collector looking for a particular deck and willing to pay your price. It may pay to wait, but if you must sell quickly, be prepared to take less."*

The demand for old and rare playing cards far exceeds the supply, and we have all experienced regret on occasion or not paying the additional dollars necessary to purchase a scarce deck that we have not had another chance to buy.

As stated earlier, it is important to remember when using the Price Guide, that it is only a guide. It is also only our opinion, which is nonetheless based on years of research, constant study of prices realized at sales and auctions, and our general experience gained in almost 30 years of collecting. We also prevailed upon a number of collectors to add their knowledge and expertise to this process in their areas of specialization. The result, we believe, is a reliable and fair guide to values as at the time of issue.

All prices are based on complete decks, with Jokers if so issued, and in the original boxes, if sold boxed. Any faults or defects, of course, reduce the value and decks in "mint plus" or "as issued" condition will almost always bring a premium.

A final point. We believe, like Gene did, that values for good decks will only rise. Scarce items only become scarcer, and as more people realize the joy of collecting playing cards and become serious collectors, the demand for old and rare decks, especially those in excellent or better condition, will continue to grow and drive prices upward.

Tom & Judy Dawson

The New York Consolidated Card Company

226 West 14th Street, New York.

TRADE DISCOUNT FROM JANUARY 1st, 1891, TO JUNE 30th, 1891.

$500 On all orders of $500 and upward,	and all subsequent purchases	25 per cent
$250- " " $250	" " "	20 "
6 Gross- " " under $250 and not less than 6 gross,	" " "	15 "
Less than 6 Gross,		List Price Net

An additional discount of 1 per cent. if paid within 10 days from the date of Invoice.
Case, Cartage and Strapping at the rate of 15 cents per gross.

To PREVENT ERRORS, please retain this Price List, and order by NUMBERS ONLY.
☞ ALL PREVIOUS PRICES AND TERMS ARE HEREBY ANNULLED.

JANUARY 1, 1891.
WHOLESALE PRICE LIST.

Lawrence & Cohen.   **John J. Levy.**
Samuel Hart & Co.

HART'S SQUEEZERS.

Trade Mark.			Per Gross.
No. 218 STEAMBOATS	Square Corners		$6 00
" 220 "	Round "		7 00
" 444 Hart's "Crown," Fancy Backs	Round "		12 00
" 23 LINEN MOGULS	Round "		30 00
" 28 BARCELONA, (Spanish Cards)	Square "		36 00
" 69 Mascotte Enameled, Fancy Backs,	Round "		16 00
" 69 " " " " Gilt Edge	" "		24 00
" 913 Montana Enameled, " "	"		18 00
" 40 Washington " "	" "		33 00
" 40 Washington, " " Gilt Edge	" "		42 00
" 19 "HART'S 1st QUALITY STEAMBOATS,"	Square Corners		18 00
" 319 EXTRA STEAMBOATS	Round "		24 00
" 31 SOLO,	Round "		48 00
" 32 IMPERIAL BOWER EUCHRE,	" "		48 00
" 34 PLAID BACK	" "		72 00
" 34 WHIST. FANCY BACKS, NON-SQUEEZERS	" "		72 00
" 35 Hart's Squeezers	" "		72 00
" 24 THE LUCKY POKER CARD, "California" and "Meteor" Backs	" "		72 00
" 53 Gem Improved Patent Squeezers	" "		72 00
" 37 GILT EDGE, assorted patterns in the dozen	" "		96 00
" 91 ROYAL. Illuminated Backs & Faces, Gilt Edge	" "		180 00
" 26 LINEN EAGLES	Square "		180 00
" 27 SQUARED FARO	" "		180 00

☞ SECOND QUALITY goods are sold at NET prices and are excluded from the terms of above PRICE LIST.

NYCC price list from 1891

REF. #	TITLE	MINT	EXCELLENT	VERY GOOD	NOTES
EARLY MAKERS • PAGES 9–22					
U1	Nathaniel Ford	$ 3,000	$ 2,500	$ 1,500	
U1a	Nathaniel Ford, miniature	2,200	1,800	1,100	
U1b	Amos Whitney	3,500	2,750	1,750	
U1c	William Coolidge	3,500	2,750	1,750	
U1d	Jazaniah Ford	3,500	2,750	1,750	
U1e	Joseph Ford	3,500	2,750	1,750	
U2	Thomas Crehore	1,500	1,200	750	
U3	Thomas Crehore	1,500	1,200	750	
U3a	Thomas Crehore	1,500	1,200	750	
U4	Thomas Crehore	1,500	1,200	750	
U5	Thomas Crehor	1,200	800	500	
U5a	American Manufacture	850	600	400	
U6	David Felt	3,500	2,750	1,750	
U7	Caleb Bartlett	1,500	1,200	750	
U8	American Manufacture, Bartlett	1,200	900	600	
U9	NY Manufactory, Bartlett	1,500	1,200	750	
U9a	Boston Card Factory, Bartlett	1,500	1,200	750	
U10	NY Manufactory, European	1,200	800	500	
U11	Bartlett, Transformation	3,000	2,400	1,500	
U12	Ely, Smith & Cook	1,500	1,200	750	
U12a	Geo. Cook, late Abbot & Ely	1,500	1,200	750	
U13	Bartlett, Abbot & Ely	1,500	1,200	750	
U14	Charles Bartlet	1,500	1,125	750	
U14	Charles Bartlet, Faro courts	1,000	750	500	
U15	Congress Card Manufactory, CR Hewet	2,000	1,500	1,000	
U15a	Congress Co.	1,200	900	600	
U17	Thoubboron	1,000	800	500	
U18	Continental, 1875	1,000	800	500	
U18a	Continental, SX3	2,000	1,500	1,000	
U18b	Continental, 1874	1,200	900	600	
U18c	Continental, Highest Trump	2,000	1,500	1,000	
U19	Mauger	1,200	900	600	
U19a	Mauger, one way Courts	1,650	1,200	850	
U19b	Mauger, 1876	2,400	1,800	1,200	
U19c	Columbias	700	500	350	
U26	Regenstein & Rosling	500	350	250	
U26a	Regenstein & Scwartz	1,000	800	500	
U27	Strauss & Trier	1,500	1,200	750	
U28	A. Ball & Bro.	300	225	150	
U29	J.Y. Humphreys	3,500	2,750	1,750	
U29a	J.Y. Humphreys	2,600	2,000	1,500	
U29b	J.Y. Humphreys	3,500	2,750	1,750	
U29c	J.Y. Humphreys	3,500	2,750	1,750	
U29d	J.Y. Humphreys, Spanish	1,800	1,400	900	
U30	Jones & Co.	1,350	1,000	675	
U31	Samuel M. Stewart	1,500	1,200	750	
U32	Robert Sauzade	2,000	1,500	1,200	
		ALL PRICES IN U.S. DOLLARS		

REF. #	TITLE	MINT	EXCELLENT	VERY GOOD	NOTES
U33	John Casenave	$ 3,000	$ 2,400	$ 1,500	
U34	Emporium	2,000	1,600	1,200	
U34a	E Pluribus Unum	1,500	1,200	900	
U35	Carmichael, Jewett, & Wales	2,000	1,600	1,000	
U36	Carmichael, Jewett, & Wales, miniature	1,500	1,200	750	
U37	Sterling Card Co.	2,000	1,600	1,000	
U38	Decatur Victory	2,000	1,500	1,000	
U39	Highlanders	2,000	1,500	1,000	
U40	Geography	2,500	2,000	1,250	
LONGLEY • PAGES 23–44					
L1	Great Mogul	2,200	1,500	1,200	
L2	Great Mogul	2,200	1,500	1,200	
L3	Great Mogul	1,800	1,300	900	
L4	Steamboat, Eagle	2,200	1,500	1,200	
L5	Eagle Card Co., Cincinnati	1,800	1,300	850	
L6	Eagle Card Co., Middletown	1,800	1,300	850	
L7	Eagle Card Co., Middletown	1,800	1,300	850	
L8	United States Card Co.	1,600	1,200	800	
L9	American PCC, New York	1,300	900	650	
L10	American PCC, New York	1,000	650	400	
L10a	Newport Steamboats	1,000	650	400	
L10b	American PCC, New York	900	600	400	
L11	Broadway Steamboats #228	900	600	400	
L12	American PCC, New York	1,200	800	500	
L13	Centennial	7,500	6,000	4,000	
L14	Border Index	3,000	2,250	1,500	
L14a	Border Index	3,000	2,250	1,500	
L15	Whist and Poker #175	3,000	2,250	1,500	
L16	Royal Flush, Card Fabrique.	1,000	750	500	
L17	Euchre, Card Fabrique	600	450	300	
L17a	Boudoirs	1,300	900	600	
L18	Union Club Card Co.	750	550	375	
L18a	Grimaud	800	600	400	
L19	Steamboats #5, Globe PCC	650	500	325	
L20	4-11-44, Globe, Middletown	550	400	300	
L21	Frederick Bold	800	600	400	
L22	4-11-44, Card Fabrique	450	325	225	
L22a	4 11-44, Globe, New York & Chicago	450	325	225	
L23	Climax #55	1,000	750	500	
L23a	Chicago-American Card Co.	500	375	250	
L24	Rough Riders #90	1,200	900	600	
L24a	Clippers	500	375	250	
L25	Good Luck #120, Chicago Card Co.	900	750	500	
L25a	Floral	900	750	500	
L25b	Crescent Card Co.	800	600	400	
L25c	Hawley Card Co.	800	600	400	
L26	Steamboat #222	750	550	375	
		ALL PRICES IN U.S. DOLLARS			

REF. #	TITLE	MINT	EXCELLENT	VERY GOOD	NOTES
L27	American Beauty #444	$ 500	$ 375	$ 250	
L27a	Xray #555	750	550	375	
L28	Layton & Co.	800	600	400	
L28a	Novelty, Wm. Hobkirk	800	600	400	
L28b	Novelty, M. F. Milward	650	450	300	
L28c	Novelty, Western	150	115	75	
L29	Steamboats #66	650	500	325	
L29a	Good Luck #120, Excelsior	650	500	325	
L30	Excelsior PCC	800	600	400	
L31	Excelsior PCC	800	600	400	
L32	League	700	550	350	
L32a	Chip Cards	850	600	400	
L33	Caterson & Brotz	400	300	200	
L34	Rough Backs	500	375	250	
L35	Imperial #96	400	300	200	
L35a	Imperial #96	600	450	300	
L36	Novelty, Caterson & Brotz	700	525	350	
L37	Reynolds Card Manufacturing	500	375	250	
L37a	Rough Back, Reynolds	500	375	250	
L38	Brooklyn PCC	600	450	300	
L38a	Knickerbocker	400	300	200	
L39	Blackstone PCC	600	450	300	
L39a	Blackstone PCC	400	300	250	
L40	Traveller's Companion	400	300	250	
L41	Union PCC	700	525	350	
L42	Squared Pharo	1,000	800	500	
L43	Union PCC	750	550	375	
L43a	Concordant	600	450	300	
L43b	Graphic	600	450	300	
L44	Union, Bernard Dreyfuss	450	340	225	
L45	Empire PCC	450	325	225	
L46	Sporting Cards, Empire	800	600	400	
L47	Sporting Cards, Union	800	600	400	
L48	Eureka, Union PCC	750	550	400	
L48a	Eureka	500	375	250	
L49	Eureka PCC	700	525	350	
L50	Paper Fabrique, Basic City	650	500	325	
L51	New Chicago PCC	550	400	275	
L52	American PCC	850	650	425	
L52a	Steamboats	800	600	400	
L53	Steamboats #99	325	225	175	
L54	Faro	750	575	400	
L55	Eagles	300	225	150	
L56	Premier #50	175	135	90	
L57	Golf #98	300	225	150	
L57a	Golfette #53	250	200	125	
L58	Rivals #15	225	175	115	
L59	Kazoo #4	200	150	100	
		ALL PRICES IN U.S. DOLLARS			

REF. #	TITLE	MINT	EXCELLENT	VERY GOOD	NOTES
L60	Bengals #11	$ 350	$ 250	$ 175	
L61	4-11-44 #18	350	250	175	
L62	Rovers #20	250	200	125	
L63	Derby #30	350	275	175	
L64	Solo #21	150	100	75	
L65	Double Pinochle #640	75	60	40	
L66	Spanish	250	200	125	
L67	Lone Hand	125	100	65	
L68	Senators #40	175	125	90	
L69	Elks #40	200	150	100	
L70	Sportingmans #45	500	400	300	
L71	Columbian #92	350	275	175	
L72	Braille	75	60	40	
L73	Foster Engineering	200	150	100	
L74	Rad-Bridge	75	60	40	
L75	Bailey, Banks & Biddle	75	60	40	
L75a	A. I. Jones	75	60	40	
L76	Brownie #35	300	225	150	
L77	American Whist League	200	150	100	
L77a	Duplicate Whist #16	75	60	40	
L78	Peter Pan	40	30	20	
L79	F. Bold	100	75	50	
L80	Detroit Card Co.	125	95	65	
L81	Rivals #1110, Columbia PCC	150	115	75	
L82	Columbia PCC	300	225	150	
NYCC • PAGES 45–66					
NY1	L.I. Cohen, 1833	1,800	1,400	900	
NY1a	L.I. Cohen, 1832	1,500	1,200	750	
NY2	L.I. Cohen, 1835	1,500	1,100	700	
NY3	Highlanders	1,500	1,100	700	
NY4	L.I. Cohen, 1840	1,200	900	600	
NY4a	L.I. Cohen, 1850	800	600	400	
NY5	Illuminated	3,000	2,000	1,500	
NY6	Illuminated	3,000	2,000	1,500	
NY6a	Illuminated	2,500	1,600	1,200	
NY7	L.I. Cohen, Spanish	500	375	250	
NY8	Lawrence, Cohen & Co.	800	600	400	
NY9	Lawrence & Cohen	600	450	300	
NY9a	Bijou	600	450	300	
NY10	Lawrence & Cohen, Illuminated	3,000	2,000	1,500	
NY11	Owen Jones	750	550	400	
NY12	Lawrence & Cohen	850	650	425	
NY13	Lawrence & Cohen	1,000	750	500	
NY14	Lawrence & Cohen, NYCC	650	450	300	
NY14a	Lawrence & Cohen, NYCC	650	450	300	
NY14b	Lawrence & Cohen, NYCC	750	550	375	
NY14c	Lawrence & Cohen	650	500	325	

ALL PRICES IN U.S. DOLLARS

REF. #	TITLE	MINT	EXCELLENT	VERY GOOD	NOTES
NY15	John J. Levy, c1845	$ 1,800	$ 1,400	$ 900	
NY16	John J. Levy, c1860, with Joker	1,250	1,000	600	
NY16a	Eagle Manfg. Co.	650	500	325	
NY16b	American Manufacture	900	675	450	
NY16b	American Manufacture, marked	1,200	900	600	
NY17	John J. Levy, c1845, war back	1,400	1,000	700	
NY17a	Steamboats	900	700	450	
NY18	Jno. J. Levy	650	500	325	
NY19	Huestis & Levy	1,400	1,100	800	
NY20	Union Card Manufactory	1,400	1,100	800	
NY20a	Union Card Manufactory, Huestis & Levy	1,400	1,100	800	
NY21	Jno. J. Levy, Union Card Manufactory	1,400	1,100	800	
NY22	Jno. J. Levy, NYCC	500	350	250	
NY22a	Jno. J. Levy	500	375	250	
NY23	Jno. J. Levy	400	300	200	
NY23a	Jno. J. Levy, NYCC	500	375	250	
NY24	Samuel Hart & Co., 1858	450	350	250	
NY24	Samuel Hart & Co.- unusual courts	1,500	1,200	800	
NY25	Hart miniatures	600	450	300	
NY26	Hart, German courts	600	450	300	
NY27	Samuel Hart & Co., c1864	400	300	200	
NY27a	American Manufacture	600	450	300	
NY27b	Henry Cohen & Co.	1,000	750	500	
NY28	Samuel Hart & Co., c1860	400	300	200	
NY29	Samuel Hart & Co., c1860	400	300	200	
NY29a	Samuel Hart & Co., c1855	450	350	225	
NY30	Samuel Hart, 1849	650	500	325	
NY31	Illuminated	3,000	2,000	1,500	
NY31a	Illuminated	5,000	3,500	2,500	
NY31b	Illuminated, Jones & Co.	3,000	2,000	1,500	
NY32	George & Martha Washington	800	600	400	
NY32	George & Martha Washington, Euchre	500	325	250	
NY33	G & M Washington, with Joker	1,200	900	600	
NY33a	George & Martha Washington	500	375	250	
NY34	George & Martha Washington	4,000	3,000	2,000	
NY35	Samuel Hart & Co., c1866	350	250	175	
NY36	Samuel Hart & Co., c1863	1,500	1,100	750	
NY36a	London Club Card	1,200	900	600	
NY36b	London Club Card	1,500	1,100	750	
NY37	Samuel Hart & Co., c1868	1,000	750	500	
NY38	NYCC Co., Manufactory	400	300	200	
NY38a	NYCC Co., Manufactory	400	300	200	
NY39	Samuel Hart & Co., NYCC	750	565	375	
NY40	California Poker	1,500	1,100	800	
NY41	Samuel Hart & Co., NYCC	300	225	150	
NY42	Samuel Hart & Co., Faro in box	400	300	200	
NY42	Samuel Hart & Co., 2 way courts	200	150	100	
		ALL PRICES IN U.S. DOLLARS			

REF. #	TITLE	MINT	EXCELLENT	VERY GOOD	NOTES
NY42a	New Development Co.	$ 20	$ 15	$ 10	
NY42b	American Manufacture	200	150	100	
NY43	Samuel Hart & Co., NYCC	250	175	125	
NY44	Saladee's Patent	2,500	2,000	1,250	
NY45	Samuel Hart & Co., Squeezers #37	300	225	150	
NY46	NYCC	350	265	175	
NY46a	Patent Squeezers	350	265	175	
NY46b	Squeezers	400	300	200	
NY46c	American Manufacture	400	300	200	
NY47	Patent Squeezers	400	300	200	
NY47a	Patent Squeezers #19	650	500	325	
NY48	Patent Squeezers	300	225	150	
NY48	Patent Squeezers, special back	600	450	350	
NY49	Squeezers #35	125	95	65	
NY50	Hart's Squeezers	20	15	10	
NY50a	#319 Squeezers Steamboats	100	75	50	
NY50b	#2 Steamboat	100	75	50	
NY50c	Ruby Queen	150	115	75	
NY51	Triton #42	125	95	65	
NY52	Gem	75	60	40	
NY53	Monaco	1,500	1,200	750	
NY54	Falstaff (Shakespearian)	350	275	175	
NY54a	Ranger (Shakespearian)	350	275	175	
NY54b	Othello (Shakespearian)	350	275	175	
NY54c	Steamboats #5	400	300	200	
NY55	Medieval	2,000	1,600	1,100	
NY56	Mascotte #69	50	40	25	
NY57	Squeezer and Trip, early	60	45	30	
NY58	Oriole #912	500	350	250	
NY59	Century #191	150	115	75	
NY60	Bee #92, c1890	200	150	100	
NY60	Bee #92, c1925	40	30	20	
NY61	Automobile #192, special Joker	450	350	225	
NY62	DeLuxe #342	100	75	50	
NY62a	DeLuxe #142	50	40	25	
NY63	Elf #93	25	20	15	
NY64	Hart's French Whist #96	40	30	20	
NY65	Bee French Whist #68	40	30	20	
Ny65a	Bee Bridge Whist #68	35	30	20	
NY66	Free Lance #915	80	60	40	
Ny66a	Free Lance #915	40	30	20	
NY66b	Free Lance #915	100	75	50	
NY67	Bee Bridge	35	30	20	
NY68	Sterling Whist #196	75	60	40	
NY69	Samuel Hart & Co., NYCC, narrow	20	15	10	
NY70	Drummer	100	75	50	
NY71	Hustler #94	100	75	50	
NY72	Uwinna	100	75	50	
		ALL PRICES IN U.S. DOLLARS			

REF. #	TITLE	MINT	EXCELLENT	VERY GOOD	NOTES
NY73	A1 The Best	$ 125	$ 95	$ 65	
NY74	Fan-Tan	100	75	50	
NY75	Carleton #919	175	135	90	
NY75a	Carleton #919	125	95	65	
NY76	Hart's Crown #4444	175	135	90	
NY77	Nestor	125	80	60	
NY78	Canary #911	50	35	25	
NY79	Monte Carlo #11	60	45	30	
NY79a	Monaco #1909	60	45	30	
NY80	Monogram Squeezers #335	50	40	25	
NY81	Lighthouse #922	125	95	65	
NY81a	Lighthouse #927 Pinochle	35	25	15	
NY82	Bailey, Banks & Biddle	30	25	15	
NY82a	Bailey, Banks & Biddle, Kaiser	125	95	65	
NY82b	Bailey, Banks & Biddle	40	30	20	
NY83	George B. Hurd	75	60	40	
NY83a	George B. Hurd	50	40	25	
NY84	Spanish Squeezers	125	95	65	
NY85	Spanish	200	150	100	
NY86	Franco-American #112	40	30	20	
NY87	Naipes Finos #28	110	85	55	
DOUGHERTY • PAGES 67–80					
AD1	Cliff St, odd courts	1,700	1,400	850	
AD1a	American Cards	2,000	1,600	1,000	
AD1b	Cliff St.	1,200	900	600	
AD1c	Cliff St., Faro courts	1,400	1,000	700	
AD1d	Beekman St., early	1,200	900	600	
AD1e	U.S. Card Manufactory	4,500	3,250	2,250	
AD1f	Cougherty & Dougherty	2,000	1,600	1,000	
AD2	Excelsior, Beekman St.	800	600	400	
AD2a	Excelsior, Beekman St., two way	700	500	350	
AD3	Illuminated	2,500	1,800	1,250	
AD4	Excelsior, Beekman St., later	600	450	300	
AD4a	Excelsior, Marked	1,600	1,200	800	
AD5	Excelsior, Beekman St., later	450	350	250	
AD6	Beekman, Latest	450	350	250	
AD7	Excelsior, Center St.	200	150	100	
AD7	Excelsior, Center St., special back	350	275	200	
AD8	Great Mogul, Center St.	400	300	200	
AD9	Excelsior, Center St., later	400	300	200	
AD10	Excelsior, Center St., later	300	225	150	
AD11	Triplicate #18	600	450	300	
AD12	Triplicate #18	600	450	300	
AD12a	Triplicate #18	800	600	400	
Ad12b	Triplicate fore-runner	750	600	375	
AD13	Double Patent Triplicate	650	500	350	
AD14	American, no indices	200	150	100	
		ALL PRICES IN U.S. DOLLARS			

REF. #	TITLE	MINT	EXCELLENT	VERY GOOD	NOTES
AD14a	American, indices	$ 150	$ 115	$ 75	
AD15	Indicator	75	60	40	
AD15a	Indicator #50	75	60	40	
AD15b	Indicator #14	200	150	100	
AD15c	Indicator #14, narrow	35	25	15	
AD16	Jewel #95	125	90	65	
AD16a	Jewel #95	125	90	65	
AD16b	Polo #80	250	190	125	
AD17	Tournament Whist #63	50	35	25	
AD17a	Tournament Whist #63	50	35	25	
AD18	Bridge Whist #45	40	30	20	
AD19	Bridge #45	30	25	15	
AD20	Bridge #345	20	15	10	
AD21	Patented	200	150	100	
AD21a	Patented, indices	150	120	80	
Ad21b	Spanish-American	300	225	150	
AD22	Tally-Ho #9	40	30	20	
AD23	Steamboats #0	200	150	100	
AD24	Steamboats #0	150	100	75	
AD25	Naipes Finos #49	200	150	100	
AD26	Naipes Superiores	150	115	75	
AD27	Klondike #4711	450	350	225	
AD28	Fair Play	300	225	150	
AD29	Outing #17	300	225	150	
AD30	Outing #17	150	115	75	
AD31	Outing #17	100	75	50	
AD32	Red Seal #16	100	75	50	
AD32a	Red Seal Piquet #161	75	60	40	
AD32b	Red Seal #16	75	60	40	
AD33	Red Seal Pinochle #016	40	30	20	
AD34	Cruiser #96	350	250	175	
AD34a	Cruiser #96	300	225	150	
AD35	Pegulose	50	40	25	
AD35a	Pegulose	30	25	15	
AD36	Empire #97	150	115	75	
AD36a	Empire #97	100	75	50	
AD37	Climax #14	100	75	50	
AD38	Double Pinochle #78	50	35	25	
AD39	Hungarian #32	100	75	50	
AD40	Marguerite #130	40	30	20	
AD41	Moon #1	60	45	30	
AD41a	Moon #1, Wide	100	75	50	
AD42	Moon Pinochle #7	40	30	20	
AD42	Hockey #7, pictured Joker	300	225	150	
AD43	Sebago Pinochle #226	60	45	30	
AD43a	Sebago	200	150	100	
AD44	American Whist League #109	300	225	150	
AD45	Rad-Bridge #201	30	25	15	
		ALL PRICES IN U.S. DOLLARS			

REF. #	TITLE	MINT	EXCELLENT	VERY GOOD	NOTES
AD46	Turtle	$ 75	$ 60	$ 40	
AD47	Waldorf #230	175	125	90	
AD48	D #8	300	225	150	
AD49	Monitor	300	225	150	
AD50	Comet	125	100	70	
AD51	Pilot #5	250	190	125	
AD51a	#000 Steamboat	250	200	125	
AD51b	Eagle Card Compy.	250	200	125	
AD51c	Eagle Card Compy.	400	300	200	
AD52	Wireless #117	80	60	40	
AD53	Plate Ace Euchre	400	300	200	
AD54	Manhattan Whist	350	250	175	
USPC • PAGES 81–107					
US1	Tigers #101, R&M	400	300	200	
US1a	Tigers #101, USPn	650	500	325	
US1b	Tigers #101, RM Fact.	200	150	100	
US1c	Tigers #101, USPC	175	125	75	
US1d	Tigers #101, RM Fact.	175	125	75	
US2	Sportsman's #202, R&M	650	500	325	
US2	Sportsman's #202, R&M, rare Joker	1,000	750	600	
US2a	Sportsman's #202, RMP	500	375	250	
US2b	Sportsman's #202, RM Fact.	125	95	65	
US2c	Sportsman's #202, Series A	125	95	65	
US2d	Sportsman's #202, RM Fact.	75	60	40	
US2e	Sportsman's #202, USPC	25	20	15	
US3	Army #303, R&M	800	625	425	
US3a	Army #303, R&M	600	450	300	
US3b	Army #303, R&M, 1981 reprint	50	40	25	
US4	Navy #303, R&M	800	625	425	
US4a	Navy #303, R&M	600	450	300	
US4b	Navy #303, R&M, 1981 reprint	50	40	25	
US5	Army & Navy #303, R&M	650	500	325	
US5a	Army & Navy #303, RMP	650	500	325	
US5b	Army & Navy #303, RMP	650	500	325	
US5c	Army & Navy #303, USPn	150	115	75	
US5d	Army & Navy #303, RM Fact.	150	115	75	
US5e	Army & Navy #303, RM Fact.	125	95	65	
US5f	Army & Navy #303, USPC	125	95	65	
US5g	Army & Navy #303, USPC	125	95	65	
US5h	Army & Navy #3032, USPC	125	95	65	
US6	Congress #404, R&M	800	600	400	
US6	Congress #606, R&M	500	350	250	
US6a	Congress #404, RMP	800	600	400	
US6a	Congress #606, RMP	300	225	150	
US6b	Congress #606, USPn	125	95	65	
US6c	Congress #606, RM Fact.	100	75	50	
US6c	Same, matching Joker	300	225	150	
US6cc	Congress #606, RM Fact.	125	95	65	
		ALL PRICES IN U.S. DOLLARS			

REF. #	TITLE	MINT	EXCELLENT	VERY GOOD	NOTES
US6d	Congress #606, USPC	$ 100	$ 75	$ 50	
US6e,f,g	Congress #606, RM Fact.	75	60	40	
US6h	Congress #606, narrow	35	30	20	
US6i	Congress #606, narrow	20	15	10	
US6m	Congress #606, modern	20	15	10	
US6n	Congress #666 Multi	1,000	750	500	
US7	Steamboat #999, R&M	400	300	200	
US7-j	Steamboat #999, R&M	350	250	200	
US7a	Steamboat #999, USPn	700	550	350	
US7a-j	Steamboat #999, USPn	700	550	350	
US7b	Steamboat #999, RM Fact.	75	60	40	
US7c	Steamboat #999, RM Fact.	40	30	20	
US7d	Steamboat #999, USPC	40	30	20	
US7e	Steamboat #999, USPC	25	20	15	
US8	Bicycle #808, RMP	450	350	225	
US8	Bicycle #808, RMP, Low Wheel Joker	500	375	250	
US8	Bicycle #808, RMP, rare colored Joker	1,500	1,100	800	
US8	Bicycle #808, RMP, Krupp	500	375	250	
US8a	Bicycle #808, RMP	500	375	250	
US8aa	Bicycle #808, USPn	500	375	250	
US8b	Bicycle #808, RM Fact.	150	100	75	
US8c	Bicycle #808, RM Fact.	50	40	25	
US8c	Bicycle #808, RM Fact., War Series	1,200	900	600	
US8d	Bicycle #808, USPC	50	40	25	
US8e	Bicycle #808, USPC	20	15	10	
US8f	Bicycle Bridge #86	15	15	10	
US8fa	Bicycle Bridge #86	15	15	10	
US8g	Bicycle Bridge #86	15	15	10	
US8h	Bicycle #88	15	15	10	
US8i	Bicycle Pinochle #48	15	15	10	
US8ia	Bicycle Pinochle #49	15	15	10	
US8j	Bicycle Jumbo #808	15	15	10	
US8k	Bicycle Bridge #888	15	15	10	
US9	Tourists #155, RMP	500	375	250	
US9a	Tourists #155, RM Fact.	150	115	75	
US9b	Tourists #155, USPC	75	60	40	
US9c	Tourists #155, RM Fact.	75	60	40	
US10	Capitol #188, RMP	300	225	150	
US10a	Capitol #188, USPC	200	150	100	
US10b	Capitol #188, RM Fact.	125	95	65	
US10c	Capitol #188, RM Fact.	125	95	65	
US10d	Capitol #188, RM Fact.	125	95	65	
US11	Squared Faro #366	750	550	300	
US12	Cabinet #707, RMP	350	250	175	
US12a	Cabinet #707, RMP	350	250	175	
US12b	Cabinet #707, USPC	150	115	75	

ALL PRICES IN U.S. DOLLARS

REF. #	TITLE	MINT	EXCELLENT	VERY GOOD	NOTES
US12c	Cabinet #707, narrow	$ 60	$ 45	$ 30	
US12d	Cabinet #707x, USPC	150	115	75	
US12e	Cabinet Bridge #707	35	30	20	
US12f	Auction Bridge #707	40	30	20	
US13	Texan #45, RMP	450	350	225	
US13-1	Texan #45, USPn	450	350	225	
US13a	Texan #45, USPn	250	190	125	
US13b	Texan #45, USPC	25	20	15	
US13c	Texan #45, 1984 repro	10	10	5	
US14	Skat #2, German Faces	125	95	65	
US15	Skat #4, American Faces	450	325	225	
US16	Ivory #93, RM Fact.	100	75	50	
US16a	Ivory Whist #93, USPn	60	45	30	
US16b	Ivory Whist #93, USPn	60	45	30	
US16c	Ivory Bridge #93, RM Fact.	50	40	25	
US16d	Ivory Pinochle #930, RM Fact.	40	30	20	
US16e	Ivory Pinochle #930, RM Fact.	35	30	20	
US16f	Ivory Pinochle #930, RM Fact.	30	25	15	
US16g	Ivory Pinochle #930, USPC	20	15	10	
US16h	Bridge #93	30	25	15	
US17	Gaigel	100	75	50	
US18-1	Treasury #89, RMP	600	450	300	
US18-2	Treasury #89, USPn	200	150	100	
US18a	Treasury #89, RM Fact.	75	60	40	
US18b	Treasury #89 Club Series, RM Fact.	75	60	40	
US18c/d	Treasury #89, Series A and B	60	45	30	
US18e	Treasury #89, RM Fact.	60	45	30	
US18f	Treasury #89 Club Solo, RM Fact.	75	60	40	
US18g	Treasury #89 Club Series, RM Fact.	75	60	40	
US18h	Treasury #89, USPC	50	40	25	
US18i	Treasury #892, RM Fact.	60	45	30	
US19	Trophy Whist #39	90	65	40	
US19a	Trophy Whist #39	50	40	25	
US19b	Trophy Bridge #39	50	40	25	
US20	New Era #46	700	550	400	
US20a	New Era #47	700	550	400	
US21	Circus #47	1,000	800	500	
US21a	Circus #47	1,000	800	500	
US22	Mystic #888	400	300	200	
US23	Pinochle #48	40	30	20	
US23a	Pinochle #48	25	20	15	
US24	Pinochle #64	25	20	15	
US25	Norwood #85	4,000	3,000	2,000	
US26	Junior #21	1,200	900	600	
US27	Petite #21	175	135	90	
US28	Initial #54	50	40	25	
		ALL PRICES IN U.S. DOLLARS			

REF. #	TITLE	MINT	EXCELLENT	VERY GOOD	NOTES
US28a	Initial #54	$ 40	$ 30	$ 20	
US29	Canteen #515	250	175	125	
US30	Picket #515	90	70	45	
US30a	Picket #515	75	60	40	
US31	Victors #79	350	250	175	
US31a	Victor #79	200	150	100	
US32	Pennant #252	125	95	65	
US32a	Pennant #253	75	60	40	
US33	Helmet #119	200	150	100	
US33a	Helmet #19	200	150	100	
US34	Jumbo Index #88	40	30	20	
US35	Auction Bridge #708	35	30	20	
US36	We-They #868	35	30	20	
US37	Cadets #343, RMP	45	35	25	
US37a	Cadets #343, USPC	25	20	15	
US37b	Cadets #343, USPC	15	15	10	
US38	Fauntleroy #29, RMP	20	15	10	
US38a	Fauntleroy #29, USPC	20	15	10	
US38b	Fauntleroy #29, USPC	10	10	5	
US39	Little Duke #24	20	15	10	
US39a	Little Duke #24	15	15	10	
US40	Fortune #814	45	35	25	
US40a	Fortune #814	45	35	25	
US41	No. 87 Bezique	75	60	40	
US42	USPC, Special	100	75	50	
US44	Oxford	70	55	35	
US45	Indian	110	85	55	
US45a	Indian	110	85	55	
US46	Hornet #6	150	110	75	
US46a	Hornet #6	20	15	10	
US47	Vogue #831	45	35	25	
US48	Owl & Spider	350	225	150	
US49	Studio	150	115	75	
US50	Double Pinochle	30	25	15	
US51	Diavolo	300	225	150	
US52	Monogram	15	15	10	
US53	Tower Mfg.	50	40	25	
US54	Senate	150	115	75	
US54a	Whist	15	15	10	
US55	United States Printing Co.	350	275	175	
US55a	Glenlivet Whisky	300	225	150	
US56	Initial Period	25	20	15	
US57	Triumph	35	30	20	
US58	Mohawk	10	10	5	
US59	Iease #801	15	15	10	
US60	Scout #108	150	115	75	

ALL PRICES IN U.S. DOLLARS

REF. #	TITLE	MINT	EXCELLENT	VERY GOOD	NOTES
NATIONAL • PAGES 108–116					
NU1	National Steamboats #9	$ 350	$ 275	$ 175	
NU2	Superior Steamboats #9	400	300	200	
NU3	Steamboat #9	300	225	150	
NU4	Owls	450	350	225	
NU4a	Owls	450	350	225	
NU5	Arrows #11	300	225	175	
NU5a	Arrows 2	350	250	175	
NU6	Aladdin #1001	300	225	175	
NU6a	Aladdin #1001	150	115	75	
NU6b	Aladdin #1001	50	40	25	
NU6c	Aladdin #1004	100	75	50	
NU7	Ramblers #22	250	175	125	
NU7a	Ramblers #22	125	95	65	
NU7b	Ramblers #22	100	75	50	
NU7c	Ramblers #22	40	30	20	
NU7d	Ramblers #22	20	15	10	
NU8	Apollo #33	400	300	200	
NU8-1	Apollo #33	400	300	200	
NU8a	Apollo #33	100	75	50	
NU8b	Apollo #33	60	45	30	
NU9	Pinochle #300	40	30	20	
NU9a	Pinochle #300	20	15	10	
NU10	Columbia #133	50	40	25	
NU10a	Columbia #133	50	40	25	
NU10b	Columbia #133, USPC	30	25	15	
NU10c	Columbia #133, Bridge	30	25	15	
NU11	Crescent #44	400	300	200	
NU12	Boston #55	150	115	75	
NU12a	Boston #55, Series A	125	95	65	
NU13	Full House Poker Cards #500	65	50	35	
NU13a	#500	20	15	10	
NU13b	#500	10	10	5	
NU13c	#500	10	10	5	
NU13d	#500	30	25	15	
NU14	Tennis #144	200	150	100	
NU15	Tennis #145, Brownie Joker	300	225	150	
NU15	National Whist #175	40	30	20	
NU15a	National Whist #175	40	30	20	
NU16	Lenox #67	350	275	175	
NU16a	Lenox #67	225	175	125	
NU17	El Dorado #49	400	300	200	
NU18	Bijou #1	125	95	65	
NU18a	Bijou #1	125	95	65	
Nu18b	Bijou #1	125	95	65	
NU19	National Club #75	200	150	100	
NU19a	National Club #752	200	150	100	
NU20	American Whist League	75	60	40	
		ALL PRICES IN U.S. DOLLARS			

REF. #	TITLE	MINT	EXCELLENT	VERY GOOD	NOTES
PERFECTION • PAGES 117–120					
PU1	Tip Top #350	$ 500	$ 375	$ 250	
PU1a	Tip Top #350	350	250	175	
PU2	Tip Top #350	150	110	80	
PU3	Steamboats #90	500	400	250	
PU4	Leader #325	300	225	150	
PU5	Steamboats #90	400	300	200	
PU5a	Roosters #100	350	275	175	
PU6	Geographical Euchre	800	600	400	
PU7	Champion #400	500	375	250	
PU8	Monarch #365	200	150	100	
PU8a	Perfection #450	350	250	175	
PU9	Perfection, London	500	375	250	
PU10	Perfection, New York	300	225	150	
PU11	Champion #400	500	375	250	
PU12	Columbus	750	550	350	
PU13	Boxer	250	190	125	
PU14	Eire #57	250	190	125	
PU15	Rooster #38	350	275	175	
PU16	Perfection, Chicago	400	300	200	
PU17	Diamond Card Co.	400	300	200	
PU17a	Diamond Card Co.	400	300	200	
PU18	Manhattan Card Co.	250	190	125	
PU19	Valley City	400	300	200	
PYRAMID • PAGES 121–123					
PY1	Winner	50	40	25	
PY2	Special	30	25	15	
PY3	Mutual	40	30	20	
PY4	Home Run	60	45	30	
PY5	Iris	35	30	20	
PY6	Pyramid #100	350	275	175	
PY6a	Pyramid #100	350	275	175	
PY6b	Pyramid #100	50	40	25	
PY7	Blue Nile	35	30	20	
PY7a	Peter Pan	125	95	65	
PY8	Blue Star	35	30	20	
PY8a	Princess	35	30	20	
PY9	Umpire	60	45	30	
PY9a	Umpire, USPC	50	40	25	
PY10	A.A.O.N.M.S.	175	130	90	
PY11	Sunbeam	35	30	20	
PY12	Barsa B	50	40	25	
RUSSELL • PAGES 124–136					
RU1	Russell's Recruits	400	300	200	
RU1a	Russell's Recruits	200	150	100	
RU2	Russell's Regents	175	125	75	
RU3	Russell's Rustlers	350	250	175	
		ALL PRICES IN U.S. DOLLARS			

REF. #	TITLE	MINT	EXCELLENT	VERY GOOD	NOTES
RU4	Russell's Pinochle	$ 130	$ 100	$ 65	
RU5	Russell's Regulars	350	275	175	
RU5a	Russell's Regulars, Skat	150	115	75	
RU5b	Rattlers	300	225	150	
RU6	Russell's Mogul	250	190	125	
RU6a	Club Mogul	250	190	125	
RU6b	Mogul #100	200	150	100	
RU7	Russell's Retrievers #40	300	225	150	
RU8	Russell's Blue Ribbon #323	450	350	225	
RU8a	Blue Ribbon	20	15	10	
RU8b	Blue Ribbon	10	10	5	
RU8c	Squared Dealers #23	800	600	400	
RU8d	Blue Ribbon	20	15	10	
RU8e	Roulette Cards	175	135	90	
RU9	Steamboat #666	450	350	225	
RU9a	Steamboat #667	400	300	200	
RU10	Strollers #04	250	190	125	
RU10a	Strollers #04, Lily	250	190	125	
RU10b	Strollers #04	250	175	125	
RU11	Success #28	400	300	200	
RU12	Kalamazoo	100	75	50	
RU13	Smart Set #400	50	35	25	
RU14	American Bank Note #502	75	60	40	
RU15	American Bank Note, German size	250	200	125	
RU16	Whist #454, Alice backs	75	60	40	
RU17	Russell	25	20	15	
RU18	Russell	20	15	10	
RU19	Aristocrat	10	10	5	
RU20	Steamboat #7-11	150	115	75	
RU21	Lily	350	250	150	
RU21a	Lily Steamboat #66	300	225	150	
RU22	Cricket	200	150	100	
RU22a	Cricket, Lily	150	115	75	
RU23	Chancellor Club #228	200	150	100	
RU23a	Chancellor Club #228	200	150	100	
RU24	Pinochle #966	80	60	40	
RU25	Bismarck Pinochle #148	150	115	75	
RU26	Lilac Whist #333	100	75	50	
RU26a	Lilac Whist #151	50	40	25	
RU26b	Lilac Bridge Whist	30	25	15	
RU27	Fads & Fancies #150	70	55	35	
RU28	Square Deal #06	350	275	175	
RU29	Monte Carlo #528	350	275	175	
RU30	Magyar-Helveta #68	75	60	40	
RU31	Unserfritz Pinochle #700	50	40	25	
RU32	Goldfield	300	225	150	
RU33	Steamboat #209	300	225	150	
		ALL PRICES IN U.S. DOLLARS			

REF. #	TITLE	MINT	EXCELLENT	VERY GOOD	NOTES
RU34	Chester #77	$ 250	$ 200	$ 125	
RU35	Regal #55	250	200	125	
RU36	Fortuna	200	150	100	
RU37	Steamboat #9999	200	150	100	
RU37a	Pastime #712	80	60	40	
RU37b	St Regis #387	80	60	40	
RU37c	Universal PCC	80	60	40	
RU37d	Key	80	60	40	
RU38	Broadway #288	250	175	125	
RU38a	Prince Henry Pinochle #123	40	30	20	
RU38b	The Rouser #549	200	150	100	
STANDARD • PAGES 137–144					
SU1	Steamboats #900	450	350	225	
SU2	Standard	150	115	75	
SU3	Steamboats #900	40	30	20	
SU4	Society #1000	50	40	25	
SU5	Airship #909	100	75	50	
SU5	Airship #909, special Joker	300	225	150	
SU5a	Fast Mail #44	80	60	40	
SU6	Native Land Series #2000	450	350	225	
SU7	American Beauty #3333	20	15	10	
SU7a	American Beauty #3334, wide	35	30	20	
SU8	Auction Bridge	25	20	15	
SU9	Standard	30	20	15	
SU9a	Aviator	20	15	10	
SU9b	Standard, generic	60	45	30	
SU9c	Standard, generic	75	60	40	
SU10	Buster #10	65	50	35	
SU11	Jap #20	20	15	10	
SU12	Lido	20	15	10	
SU13	Austen Beauties #506	350	275	175	
SU13a	Austen Beauties #506	350	275	175	
SU14	J. I. Austen	400	300	200	
SU14a	Buffet	400	300	200	
SU15	Steamboats #199 1/2	160	120	80	
SU16	Crescent PCC	300	225	150	
SU17	Albert Pick	50	40	25	
SU17a	Fastmail	60	45	30	
SU18	Bellevue	125	95	65	
SU19	Rembrandts	125	95	65	
SU21	Buckeye Card Co.	100	75	50	
SU22	Buckeye Card Co.	200	150	100	
SU23	Thistle	150	115	75	
SU23a	Whist Club #37	200	150	100	
SU23b	Thistle, narrow	15	15	10	
SU24	Bay State Card Co.	100	75	50	
SU25	Nugget J	400	300	225	

ALL PRICES IN U.S. DOLLARS

REF. #	TITLE	MINT	EXCELLENT	VERY GOOD	NOTES
SU26	Judge	$ 125	$ 75	$ 50	
SU27	Magician	200	150	100	
SU28	Bay State Card Co.	200	150	100	
SU28a	Steamboats	350	275	175	
SU29	Regal	150	115	75	
SU30	Valor	40	30	20	
SU31	Stampede #189	150	110	85	
OTHER WIDE MAKERS • PAGES 145–150					
MSW27	Astor PCC	40	30	20	
MSW75	Theodore L. DeLand	400	300	200	
MSW78	Dorrity, Pinochle #1909	200	150	100	
MSW78a	Dorrity, Steamboat #1999	400	300	200	
MSW79	Dorrity, Lucky Dog	300	225	150	
MSW79a	Continental, Lucky Dog	300	225	150	
MSW85	Empire State	300	225	150	
MSW88	Independent, metal case	175	125	85	
MSW88a	Tug-O-War Steamboat	150	115	75	
MSW89	Rex #79	150	115	75	
MSW91	Koehler, gold background	1,800	1,400	900	
MSW91a	Columbia #27	800	600	400	
MSW91b	D. Lesser	800	600	400	
MSW91c	Yale #49	800	600	400	
MSW91d	United States Card Co.	800	600	400	
MSW99	New England PCC	125	80	50	
MSW131	Midland Special	75	60	40	
MSW131a	Good Times	20	15	10	
MSW131b	Golf	30	25	15	
MSW135	Western Press	50	40	25	
MSW136	Universal	15	15	10	
MSW136a	Dauntless	40	30	20	
MSW140	Bunker Hill #1776	250	200	150	
MSW141	Atlas PCC	300	225	150	
MSW142	Overland	250	200	125	
MSW143	Rough Rider	300	225	150	
MSW144	Star	250	200	125	
NARROW • PAGES 151–162					
MSN1	Arrow PCC	25	20	15	
MSN1a	Arrco	20	15	10	
MSN1b/c	Arrco	15	15	10	
MSN1d	Arrow, generic	10	10	5	
MSN2	Service	15	15	10	
MSN3	Centaur	15	15	10	
MSN4	Arrco	5	5	5	
MSN4a	Enardoe	10	10	5	
MSN5/5a	Arrco	20	15	10	
MSN6/6a	Arrco	10	10	5	
MSN7	Arrco	20	15	10	
		ALL PRICES IN U.S. DOLLARS			

REF. #	TITLE	MINT	EXCELLENT	VERY GOOD	NOTES
MSN11	Bailey, Banks & Biddle	$ 30	$ 25	$ 15	
MSN12	Brown & Bigelow	10	10	5	
MSN13	Remembrance	10	10	5	
MSN14	Remembrance, generic	10	10	5	
MSN15	Brown & Bigelow	10	10	5	
MSN16	Kent	5	5	5	
MSN17	Fortuna	10	10	5	
MSN18	NASCO	25	20	15	
MSN19	NASCO, Spanish	60	45	30	
MSN20	NASCO	25	20	15	
MSN21	Nu Vue	10	10	5	
MSN22	Luxor	25	20	15	
MSN23	Monte Carlo	50	40	25	
MSN24	Astor	15	15	10	
MSN25	Cadigan	10	10	5	
MSN26	Cairo	25	20	15	
MSN27	Carotti	25	20	15	
MSN28	Collegiate	30	25	15	
MSN29	Criterion	30	25	15	
MSN30	Criterion	30	25	15	
MSN31	Permanite	30	25	15	
MSN32	Cruver	25	20	15	
MSN33	Zodiac	35	30	20	
MSN34	Dale	25	20	15	
MSN35	Fairco	10	10	5	
MSN36	Fairco	10	10	5	
MSN37	Kem	20	15	10	
MSN39	Gibson Slims	20	15	10	
MSN40-45	Gibsons	20	15	10	
MSN46	Challenge, wide	30	25	15	
MSN46a	Challenge, narrow	20	15	10	
MSN47-50	Gibsons	20	15	10	
MSN51	King Press	20	15	10	
MSN52	Play-Well, King Press	25	20	15	
MSN53	Play-Well, Hurley	20	15	10	
MSN54	Play-Well, Young & Rudolph	30	25	15	
MSN55	Wedgewood	30	25	15	
MSN56	Little Old New York	20	15	10	
MSN57	Godey's	20	15	10	
MSN58	Goofy	50	40	25	
MSN59	Victorian Lady	20	15	10	
MSN60	Galaxy	20	15	10	
MSN61	Mosaic	20	15	10	
MSN62	Past-l-Eze	15	15	10	
MSN63	Raggy Scot	20	15	10	
MSN64	Polka Dot	20	15	10	
MSN65	Technique	20	15	10	
		ALL PRICES IN U.S. DOLLARS			

REF. #	TITLE	MINT	EXCELLENT	VERY GOOD	NOTES
MSN66	Golden Weave	$ 15	$ 15	$ 10	
MSN67	Party	20	15	10	
MSN68	Kreko	30	25	15	
MSN69	Scamper	30	25	15	
MSN70	Thorobred	30	25	15	
MSN71	Hallmark	5	5	5	
MSN71a	Hallmark	20	15	10	
MSN72	Peau-Doux	10	10	5	
MSN73	Trinacria, Italian	60	45	30	
MSN74	Western	5	5	5	
MSN74a	Western	5	5	5	
MSN75	Contraband	30	25	15	
MSN76	USPC	30	25	15	
MSN77	Spanish Art	30	25	15	
MSN78	J. E. Caldwell	30	25	15	
MSN79	LaFrance	30	25	15	
MSN80	Charme	20	15	10	
PICTORIAL • PAGES 163–166					
Wide	Wide Brands, common	35	25	15	
Wide	Wide Brands, rarest	500	350	250	
Narrow	Narrow Brands	25	20	10	
CANADIAN STANDARD • 167–178					
CDN1	Maples	1,000	750	500	
CDN2	Burland, single-ended	500	375	250	
CDN2a	Burland, Four Corner indices	400	300	200	
CDN2b	Union, Four Corner indices	400	300	200	
CDN2c	Our Special	200	150	100	
CDN2d	Peerless	200	150	100	
CDN2e	Union, no indices	500	375	250	
CDN3	Mikado	500	375	250	
CDN4	St. Lawrence	300	225	150	
CDN5	Union, Golfer #22	600	450	350	
CDN5a	Consolidated Litho, Golfer #22	250	190	125	
CDN5b	Consolidated Litho, Golfer #23	175	140	100	
CDN6	Union, Sports Junior	200	150	100	
CDN6a	Consolidated Litho, Sports Junior	125	95	65	
CDN7	Pyramid	75	50	35	
CDN8	Colonial Bridge	100	75	50	
CDN9	Sports Bridge	60	45	30	
CDN10	International PCC	30	25	15	
CDN11	Steamboat #999, Toronto	250	190	125	
CDN11a	Steamboat #999, Windsor	150	115	75	
CDN12	Hornet #6, Toronto	50	40	25	
CDN12a	Hornet #6, Windsor	35	30	20	
CDN13	Picket #515, Toronto	50	40	25	
CDN13a	Picket #515, Windsor	35	30	20	
CDN14	Vogue #831, Toronto	75	60	40	
		ALL PRICES IN U.S. DOLLARS			

REF. #	TITLE	MINT	EXCELLENT	VERY GOOD	NOTES
CDN14a	Vogue #831, Windsor	$ 50	$ 40	$ 25	
CDN15	Bicycle #808, Toronto	100	75	50	
CDN15a	Bicycle #808, Windsor	70	55	35	
CDN15b	Bicycle Bridge #888	25	20	15	
CDN16	Texan #45, Toronto	125	95	65	
CDN16a	Texan #45, Windsor	70	55	35	
CDN16b	Texan #45, Windsor	20	15	10	
CDN17	Pinochle #48	15	15	10	
CDN18	Little Duke #24	50	40	25	
CDN19	Cadets #343	30	25	15	
CDN20	Fauntleroy #29	15	15	10	
CDN21	Rambler #22	40	30	20	
CDN21a	Rambler Whist #22w	10	10	5	
CDN22	Hart's Squeezers #352	60	45	30	
CDN23	Derby #181	20	15	10	
CDN24	Lark #123	15	15	10	
CDN24a	Rex #7	10	10	5	
CDN24b	British Consuls	35	25	15	
CDN25	Congress #606	25	20	15	
CDN26	Apollo #33	100	75	50	
CDN27	Columbia #133	60	45	30	
CDN28	Standard Card & Paper	600	450	300	
CDN29	Montreal Litho, miniature	400	300	200	
CDN30	Montreal Litho	250	200	125	
CDN30a	Canvas-back	175	135	90	
CDN31	Dominion Rubber	1,200	900	600	
CDN32	Le Trappeur	1,000	750	500	
CDN33	Empress	800	600	400	
CDN33a	Empress, insert	1,800	1,350	1,000	
CDN34	Converse, Coulson & Lamb	650	500	300	
CDN35	Tandem	700	550	350	
CDN36	Pearsall	400	300	200	
CDN36a	Pearsall, indices	350	250	150	
CDN37	Burland	700	550	350	
CDN38	Defiance #91	600	450	300	
CDN39	Royal, W, B, & R	500	400	300	
CDN40	T&B Cigarettes	250	190	125	
CDN41	Beauchemin & Valois	400	300	200	
CDN42	Canadian Card Co.	300	225	150	
ADVERTISING • PAGES 179-204					
A1	Murphy Varnish (T5)	4,000	3,000	2,000	
A2	Kinney (T8)	1,500	1,125	750	
A3	Crosscut (SE11)	2,500	1,900	1,200	
A4	Craddock's Soap (SE2)	250	190	125	
A5	Caffee, Cleveland (P3)	1,800	1,350	900	
A5a	Caffee, Harrison (P18)	2,000	1,500	1,000	
A6	Cleveland Campaign (P17)	2,000	1,500	1,000	

ALL PRICES IN U.S. DOLLARS

REF. #	TITLE	MINT	EXCELLENT	VERY GOOD	NOTES
A7	President Suspenders (P4)	$ 600	$ 450	$ 300	
A8	Goldwater (P10)	50	40	25	
A9	Anheuser-Busch (W15)	700	525	350	
A10	Anheuser-Busch (W16)	700	525	350	
A11	Pep Boys, wide	100	75	50	
A12	Monarch Bicycle	1,000	750	500	
A13	Hayner Distillery (SX11)	350	250	150	
A14	Enterprise Brewing (SX16)	500	375	250	
A15	Advertising, NYCC	250	200	150	
A16	Coca-Cola Spotter (W34)	100	75	50	
A17	Time Magazine	50	40	25	
A18	Schering	40	30	20	
A19	Coricidin	20	15	10	
A20	Springmaid	75	60	40	
A21	Ford	20	15	10	
A22	Ford, Ride & Win	20	15	10	
A23	Hamm's Bear Cards	50	40	25	
A24	Kent Military (W39)	50	40	25	
A25	Statham Catalog	25	20	15	
A26	U.S. Plywood	25	20	15	
A27	Elliot	60	45	30	
A28	Official Films (SE13)	125	95	65	
A29	Jack Daniels	10	10	5	
A30	Black Velvet	10	10	5	
A31	Universal Stars (SE14)	200	150	100	
A32	Laugh In (SE26)	25	20	15	
A33	Corfam	25	20	15	
A34	Reynolds Wrap	30	25	15	
A35	General Dynamics	50	40	25	
A36	Captain Crunch	50	40	25	
A37	Sodium Bicarbonate	50	40	25	
A38	Richardson Roller	1,800	1,400	900	
A39	Half Face Euchre	1,200	1,000	600	
A40	IBM	65	50	35	
A41	CIBA	25	20	15	
A42	Prudential	30	25	15	
A43	Schlitz	30	25	15	
A44	Computer Automation	15	15	10	
A45	Complicated Whist	600	500	300	
A46	Aerospace	20	15	10	
A47	Guthman	15	15	10	
A48	Fragrant Vanity Fair	1,200	1,000	600	
A49	Boston Merchants	2,000	1,600	1,200	
AA1	Dr. Ransom	1,000	750	600	
AA2	Grand Mackinac Hotel	1,000	750	500	
AA3	Plant System	500	400	250	
AA4	5A Horse Blanket	300	225	150	
		ALL PRICES IN U.S. DOLLARS			

REF. #	TITLE	MINT	EXCELLENT	VERY GOOD	NOTES
AA5	Buchanan & Lyle	$ 750	$ 500	$ 375	
AA6	RCA	75	60	40	
AA7	Mandel Department Store	100	75	50	
AA8	Ohio Knife, wide	250	190	125	
AA9	Ohio Knife, narrow	100	75	50	
AA10	Ladish Co.	20	15	10	
AA11	United States Graphite	300	225	150	
AB1	Tobacco	300	225	150	
AB2	Liquor	250	190	125	
AB3	Brewery	350	265	175	
AB4	Food and Drink	200	150	100	
AB5	Road Transportation	250	190	125	
AB6	Household Products	200	150	100	
AB7	Railroad and Steamship	350	265	175	
AB8	Machinery and Equipment	200	150	100	
AB9	Sports	450	325	225	
AB10	Stores	150	120	90	
AB11	Miscellaneous	200	150	100	
AB	Narrow decks, low interest	60	45	30	
AB	Narrow decks, highest interest	400	300	200	
AC	Ad Backs, Joker and XC only	150	100	75	
ADD	Ad Back and Ace only	40	30	20	
Type 6	Ad Back only	5	5	5	
AE	Oversize	50	40	25	
AF	Special packaging	250	190	125	
TRANSFORMATION • PAGES 205–208					
T1	Bartlett	2,500	1,900	1,250	
T2	Samuel Hart	2,500	2,000	1,250	
T2a	Samuel Hart, variation	2,500	2,000	1,250	
T3	Eclipse	3,500	2,700	1,750	
T4	Tiffany	1,400	1,000	750	
T5	Murphy Varnish	4,000	3,000	2,000	
T6	Kinney, Harlequin Insert	1,250	950	625	
T7	Kinney, Harlequin Insert	1,250	950	625	
T8	Kinney	1,500	1,200	750	
T9	Hustling Joe	1,000	750	500	
T10	Hustling Joe, Variation	1,000	750	500	
T11	Vanity Fair	600	450	300	
T12	Ye Witches	300	225	150	
T13	Funny Spot	3,500	2,800	2,000	
T14	Sutherland-Brown	50	40	25	
INSERT CARDS • PAGES 209–216					
I1	5 Cent Ante	2,500	1,850	1,250	
I2	Lorillard's Snuff	2,500	1,875	1,250	
I2a	Lorillard's Snuff	2,500	1,875	1,250	
I3	Hard a Port, black	1,750	1,350	875	
I4	Hard a Port, black, no logo	2,000	1,500	1,000	
		ALL PRICES IN U.S. DOLLARS			

REF. #	TITLE	MINT	EXCELLENT	VERY GOOD	NOTES
I5	Trumps Long Cut, black	$ 1,750	$ 1,350	$ 875	
I6	Kid's Plug Cut	2,000	1,500	1,000	
I7	Snipe Plug Cut	2,500	2,000	1,250	
I7a	Red Boot Long Cut	4,000	3,000	2,000	
I7b	Deep Run Hunt Club Whiskey	4,000	3,000	2,000	
I8	Kinney, Harlequin (T6)	1,250	950	625	
I9	Kinney, Harlequin (T7)	1,250	950	625	
I10	Kinney Transparent	1,250	950	625	
I11	Kinney Transparent	1,250	950	625	
I11a	Kinney Transparent	1,250	950	625	
I12	Trumps Long Cut, brown	1,250	950	625	
I13	Hard a Port, blue	1,000	750	500	
I14	Hard a Port, blue, no logo	1,500	1,100	750	
I15	Moore & Calvi	750	550	375	
I15a	Moore & Calvi, Cullingworth	750	550	375	
I15b	Moore & Calvi, MacLin-Zimmer	750	550	375	
I16	Maclin-Zimmer	750	550	375	
I17	Maclin-Zimmer-McGill	750	550	375	
I18	Maclin-Zimmer-McGill, 2 logos	1,250	900	625	
I19	Hard a Port, Blue, large circle	750	550	375	
I20	Trumps Long Cut, blue	750	550	375	
I21	W. Duke, Sons & Co., Turkish	750	550	375	
I22	W. Duke, Sons & Co.	750	550	375	
I23	Taylor Biscuit	200	150	100	
I24	Wm. S. Kimball	1,250	950	625	
I25	Wool Candy	75	60	40	
I26	Premium Slips	25	20	15	
I27	Adam's Gum, set of 10	50	40	25	
CANADIAN INSERTS • PAGES 214–216					
ICA1	McDonald's British Consols	200	150	100	
ICA2	McDonald's British Consols	150	115	75	
ICA3	McDonald's British Consols	125	95	65	
ICA4	McDonald's British Consols	200	150	100	
ICA5	McDonald's British Consols	100	75	50	
ICA6	McDonald's, War Series	125	95	65	
ICA7	McDonald's, War Series	125	95	65	
ICA8	McDonald's, War Series	125	95	65	
ICA9	Quaker Candy	100	75	50	
ICA10	D. Ritchie & Co.	2,000	1,500	1,000	
ICA10a	D. Ritchie & Co.	2,000	1,500	1,000	
ICA11	Mitchell	1,800	1,350	1,000	
WAR • PAGES 217–226					
W1	Decatur	5,000	3,500	2,500	
W2	Seminole Wars, Humphreys	14,000	9,000	7,000	
W2a	Seminole Wars, Abbot & Ely	5,000	3,500	2,500	
W2b	Seminole Wars, reproduction	20	15	10	
W3	Lafayette	5,000	3,500	2,500	

ALL PRICES IN U.S. DOLLARS

REF. #	TITLE	MINT	EXCELLENT	VERY GOOD	NOTES
W4	Mexican War	$ 2,000	$ 1,500	$ 1,000	
W4a	Mexican War II	1,000	750	500	
W5	Union	1,000	750	500	
W6	Union II, Goddesses	1,600	1,200	800	
W6a	Union II, Canteen Girls	1,750	1,350	900	
W7	Confederate Generals	4,000	3,000	2,000	
W8	Union Generals	4,000	3,000	2,000	
W9	Union Generals, National Picture	5,000	3,500	2,500	
W10	Confederate, Goodall	400	300	200	
W11	Monitor & Merrimac	6,000	4,500	3,000	
W12	Army, Russell Morgan & Co.	750	575	375	
W12a	Army, 1981 reprint	50	40	25	
W13	Navy, Russell Morgan & Co.	750	575	375	
W13a	Navy, 1981 reprint	50	40	25	
W14	Army & Navy	550	425	275	
W15	Anheuser Busch, Gray Litho	700	525	350	
W16	Anheuser Busch, USPC	700	525	350	
W17	Spanish American War	750	550	350	
W18	Dutton's Military	500	375	250	
W19	Russell's Regulars	350	275	175	
W20	Cruiser #96	350	250	175	
W21	Allied Armies	400	300	200	
W21a	Allied Armies	400	300	200	
W21b	Allied Armies	400	300	200	
W21c	Allied Armies	400	300	200	
W22a	Allied Armies	400	300	200	
W22b	Allied Armies	400	300	200	
W22c	Dominion Rubber (CDN31)	1,200	900	600	
W22d	Allied Armies	700	575	350	
W23	Liberty	800	600	400	
W24	Freedom	600	450	300	
W25	Democracy	700	500	350	
W26	Playanlern	250	200	125	
W27	Military FT	40	30	20	
W28	Bicycle #808, War Series	1,200	900	600	
W29	Grand Army of Republic	1,200	900	600	
W30	Mlle. from Armentierre	700	500	400	
W31	Submarine Deck	60	45	30	
W32	Aircraft Spotters	20	15	10	
W33	Aircraft Spotters	20	15	10	
W34	Coca-Cola Spotters	85	65	40	
W35	ANMA	40	30	20	
W35a	ANMA	40	30	20	
W36	Victory	100	75	50	
W37	Forbidden City	500	375	250	
		ALL PRICES IN U.S. DOLLARS			

REF. #	TITLE	MINT	EXCELLENT	VERY GOOD	NOTES
W38	Amerikards	$ 800	$ 600	$ 400	
W39	Kent Cigarettes	40	30	20	
W40	Militac	80	60	40	
W41	Game of Peace	200	150	100	
W42	War Scenes	2,500	2,000	1,250	
W43	Teddy Cards	800	600	400	
W44	Aviation Deck	75	60	40	
W45	Recognition Cards	60	45	30	
W46	Hunt	1,500	1,100	750	
W47	William Aiken Walker	30,000	20,000	15,000	
W48	Victors	350	250	175	
W49	Canteen	250	175	125	
W50	Picket	90	70	45	
W51	Centennial	7,500	6,000	4,000	
POLITICAL & PATRIOTIC • PAGES 227–232					
P1	George & Martha	700	525	350	
P2	Bad Joker	4,000	3,000	2,000	
P3	Caffee, Cleveland	1,800	1,350	900	
P4	President Suspender	600	450	300	
P5	Royal Revelers	150	115	75	
P5	Royal Revelers, double set	400	275	200	
P6	George Washington	300	225	150	
P7	Bannister Babies	35	30	20	
P8	Kennedy Kards	25	20	15	
P9	LBJ Texas White House	15	15	10	
P10	Goldwater AuH2O	50	40	25	
P11	Queen High Equality	25	20	15	
P12	Politicards	15	15	10	
P13	President's	40	30	20	
P14	Executive Deck	40	30	20	
P15	Votes for Women	1,000	700	500	
P15a	Votes for Women II	1,000	700	500	
P15b	Votes for Women	1,000	700	500	
P15c	Votes for Women	30	20	10	
P16	'49'	350	250	175	
P17	Cleveland Campaign	1,800	1,350	900	
P17a	Cleveland Campaign, Reprint	15	15	10	
P18	Caffee, Harrison	2,000	1,500	1,000	
P19	Time Magazine	50	40	30	
P20	Political Euchre	1,200	900	600	
P20a	Political Euchre	1,100	800	550	
P21	Socialist	2,000	1,600	1,000	
P22	Royal Illuminated	1,200	900	600	
P23	Chas. P. Hart	350	250	175	
P24	Russian Monarch	1,000	750	600	
P25	Sockem	300	225	150	
		ALL PRICES IN U.S. DOLLARS			

REF. #	TITLE	MINT	EXCELLENT	VERY GOOD	NOTES
SPORTS & ENTERTAINMENT • PAGES 233–240					
SE1	Babes in the Wood	$ 1,400	$ 1,000	$ 700	
SE2	Craddock's Soap	250	200	125	
SE3	Stage #65	125	100	75	
SE4	Stage #65	125	100	75	
SE5	Stage #65, 1908	175	135	90	
SE6	Jeffries	500	375	250	
SE7	Movies by Moriarty	100	75	50	
SE8	Baseball, 1888	20,000	13,000	10,000	
SE9	Molly O	750	500	350	
SE10	10th Olympiad	150	115	75	
SE11	Duke's Crosscut	2,000	1,500	1,000	
SE12	Baseballized	800	600	400	
SE13	Official Films	125	90	50	
SE14	Universal Stars	250	175	125	
SE15	Hollywood Fortune	100	75	50	
SE16	Baseball Backs, Russell	500	375	250	
SE17	Baseball Backs, NYCC	300	225	150	
SE18	Baseball Backs, National	200	150	100	
SE19	Home Run	60	45	30	
SE19a	Umpire	60	45	30	
SE20	Black Crook	1,500	1,100	800	
SE21	Brown Derby	30	25	15	
SE22	WC Fields	15	15	10	
SE23	Arcade Cards, 1928 full-size	250	200	125	
SE24	Man From Uncle	20	15	10	
SE25	Green Hornet	35	30	20	
SE26	Laugh-in	25	20	15	
SE27	Pop Music	15	15	10	
SE28	Country Music	15	15	10	
SE29	Monkees	20	15	10	
SE30	Baseball, miniature	10	10	5	
SE31	Personalities, miniature	10	10	5	
SE32	Western Stars	60	45	30	
SE33	Flickers	12	10	10	
SE34	NFL Greats	35	30	20	
SE35	Milwaukee Bucks, Coke	75	60	40	
SE36	Shirley Temple	85	65	45	
SE37	Movie Stars	400	300	200	
SE38	Batter Up	250	175	125	
TAROT AND FORTUNE TELLING • PAGES 241–246					
TA1	Rider-Waite, 1910/1920	5,000/500	4,500/450	4,000/400	
TA2	Adytum, 1922	100	75	50	
TA3	Knapp, 1929	500	450	400	
TA4	Green Spade, Petrtyl—78 cards/54 cards	4,000/3,800	3,500/3,300	3,000/2,700	
TA5	New Tarot for the Aquarian Age	100	90	75	
TA6	New Tarot, Hurley & Horler	50	40	25	

ALL PRICES IN U.S. DOLLARS

REF. #	TITLE	MINT	EXCELLENT	VERY GOOD	NOTES
FT1	Turner & Fisher, c1850	$ 200	$ 150	$ 100	
FT2	Le Normand	150	115	75	
FT3	Gipsy	40	30	20	
FT4	Temple of Revelation	100	75	50	
FT5	Le Normand, hand-colored	150	115	75	
FT6	Le Normand, Neilen	100	75	50	
FT7	Madam Morrow	150	115	75	
FT8	Comic Cards of Fortune	1,200	800	500	
FT9	Ye Witches	300	225	150	
FT10	Egyptian, Rost	500	375	225	
FT11	Nile Fortune	75	60	40	
FT12	Nile Fortune II	25	20	15	
FT13	Gypsy Witch	20	15	10	
FT14	Astrological Fate	200	150	100	
FT15	Revelation	40	30	20	
FT16	Military FT (W27)	40	30	20	
FT17	Wheel of Fortune	200	150	100	
FT18	Let's Tell Fortunes	100	75	50	
FT19	Sheldon's	80	60	40	
FT20	Cards of Fate, Singer	200	150	100	
FT21	Cabalistic	750	500	350	
FT22	Wizard	40	30	20	
FT23	Mme. Doerflinger	175	135	90	
FT24	Ladie Lucile	100	75	50	
FT25	Sabina	100	75	50	
EXPOSITION AND WORLD'S FAIR • PAGES 247–252					
SX1	Mauger Centennial	2,400	1,800	1,200	
SX2	Dougherty Centennial	3,000	2,400	1,500	
SX3	Continental Centennial	2,000	1,500	1,000	
SX4	Royal	1,200	900	600	
SX5	Spanish Squeezers NYCC	500	375	250	
SX6	Clark's Columbian	100	75	50	
SX7	Winter's Columbian	150	115	75	
SX8	Winter's Columbian	250	190	125	
SX8a	Columbian	200	150	100	
SX10	Harter's Columbian	500	375	250	
SX11	Hayner's Columbian	400	300	200	
SX12	Columbiano Naipes	650	500	325	
SX13	Bicycle Spanish	500	375	250	
SX13a	Bicycle Spanish	250	190	125	
SX13b	Bicycle Spanish	300	225	150	
SX14	Los Leones	125	95	65	
SX15	Midwinter	350	275	175	
SX16	Midwinter, Enterprise Brewery	700	500	350	
SX17	Paris Exposition	125	90	60	
SX18	Pan American	75	60	40	
SX19	Pan Am Aluminum	800	600	400	
		ALL PRICES IN U.S. DOLLARS			

REF. #	TITLE	MINT	EXCELLENT	VERY GOOD	NOTES
SX19a	Pan Am Aluminum, Calumet	$ 1,200	$ 900	$ 600	
SX20	St. Louis Aluminum	1,000	750	500	
SX21	Louisiana Purchase	175	130	90	
SX22	Philippine, 1904	750	550	375	
SX23	Jamestown	250	175	125	
SX24	Alaska Yukon Pacific	150	115	75	
SX25	Panama Pacific, tower	250	190	125	
SX26	Chicago, 1933	30	25	15	
SX27	Chicago, 1934	30	25	15	
SX28	Chicago, Arrco	30	25	15	
SX31	New York, 1939	40	30	20	
SX32	New York, 1939	30	25	15	
SX33	New York, Futurama	60	45	30	
SX34	Texas Centennial, Flag	35	30	20	
SX34a	Texas Centennial, Map	35	30	20	
SX34b	Texas Centennial, Star	35	30	20	
SX35	New York, 1964	15	15	10	
SX36	New York, 1939, Kem	60	45	30	
SX37	Sesquicentennial	75	60	40	
SX38	Columbian, Perfection PCC	750	550	350	
SOUVENIR • PAGES 253–264					
S1	Alaska, Mitchell	450	325	225	
S2	Alaska, Puget	125	95	65	
S3	American Indian	400	300	200	
S3a	Basket Joker	450	340	225	
S4	A Hopi Boy	2,500	1,875	1,250	
S5	Indians of the Southwest	225	180	125	
S6	Historic Boston	60	45	30	
S7	Historic Boston	40	30	20	
S8	Buffalo & Niagara	60	45	30	
S9	Maid of The Mist	150	100	75	
S10	Burro	1,250	1,000	625	
S11	California, Seal	60	45	30	
S12	California, Waters	40	30	20	
S13	California, Rieder	40	30	20	
S14	California, Rieder	75	60	40	
S15	California, Rieder	150	115	75	
S16	California, Rieder	150	115	75	
S17	California, Mission Bell	50	40	25	
S18	California, Mission Bell	50	40	25	
S19	California, Bullocks	100	75	50	
S20	Columbia River Highway	400	300	200	
S21	Florida, Tom Jones	350	275	175	
S22	Florida East Coast	25	20	15	
S23	Grand Rapids	800	600	400	
S24	Great Lakes, Western	100	75	50	
S25	Great Lakes, Eastern	150	120	75	

ALL PRICES IN U.S. DOLLARS

REF. #	TITLE	MINT	EXCELLENT	VERY GOOD	NOTES
S26	Great Southwest	$ 150	$ 115	$ 75	
S26a	Great Southwest	150	115	75	
S27	Great Southwest	150	115	75	
S28	Hawaiian	90	70	45	
S29	Hawaiian	50	40	25	
S30	Inter-Mountain, Prospector	175	135	90	
S31	Inter-Mountain, Wagon Train	175	135	90	
S32	Maine	75	60	40	
S33	Montana & Yellowstone	125	100	75	
S34	Mountain States	550	400	300	
S35	New Orleans & Gulf	175	125	90	
S36	New York City, 1900	100	75	50	
S37	New York City, 1915	50	40	25	
S37a	New York City	70	55	35	
S38	New York & Hudson River	100	75	50	
S39	New York, Bosselman	150	115	75	
S39a	New York, Standard PCC	150	115	75	
S40	Niagara Falls	70	55	35	
S41	Niagara Falls, bamboo border	700	525	350	
S42	North Shore	200	175	125	
S43	O'Callaghans, Chicago	100	75	50	
S44	Oregon	350	265	175	
S45	Panama, Inaugural	100	75	50	
S46	Panama, Royal Palms	60	45	30	
S47	Panama, Chagres River	60	45	30	
S48	Panama, Red Sky	60	45	30	
S49	Panama, Ship in Canal	125	90	65	
S50	Panama, Galleon	45	35	25	
S50a	Panama, Galleon	80	60	40	
S51	Pittsburgh, 1901	75	60	40	
S52	Pittsburgh, May Drug	75	60	40	
S53	Portland by the Sea	75	60	40	
S54	Portland & Columbia River	200	150	100	
S55	Rhode Island	100	75	50	
S56	Rocky Mountain	150	115	75	
S57	Rocky Mountain	300	225	150	
S58	Rocky Mountain	100	75	50	
S59	Rocky Mountain	75	60	40	
S60	St. Joseph	200	150	100	
S61	St. Louis	225	175	150	
S62	Texas	125	100	75	
S63	Vermont	60	45	30	
S64	Washington, Waters	125	95	65	
S65	Washington, USPC	60	45	30	
S66	Washington, Goddess	40	30	20	
S67	Washington, Bosselman	125	95	65	
S68	Washington State, 1899	125	100	70	
		ALL PRICES IN U.S. DOLLARS			

REF. #	TITLE	MINT	EXCELLENT	VERY GOOD	NOTES
S69	Washington & Pacific	$ 125	$ 100	$ 70	
S70	Washington State	125	95	65	
S71	White Mountains	50	40	25	
S72	Sea To Summit	40	30	20	
S73	Yellowstone, YNR	125	95	65	
S74	Yellowstone, Old Faithful	250	190	125	
S75	Yellowstone, Geyser Basin	50	40	25	
S76	Yosemite	60	45	30	
S77	Chicago, Bosselman	150	100	70	
S77a	Chicago, pattern back	150	100	70	
S78	Macatawa Bay	4,500	3,750	3,000	
S79	Cincinnati	2,000	1,700	1,400	
S80	Philadelphia	50	40	25	
S81	Virginia	350	250	175	
S82	Michigan	2,000	1,500	1,000	
S83	Yellowstone Park	900	650	450	
S84	Great Northwest	750	550	375	
S85	Lancaster	1,600	1,300	800	
S86	Del Coronado	2,000	1,500	1,000	
S87	Lake Tahoe	2,000	1,500	1,000	
S88	Lake Tahoe	2,000	1,500	1,000	
S89	Santa Anita	2,250	1,700	1,200	
RAILROAD SOUVENIRS • PAGES 265–268					
SR1	CM & St. P	300	225	150	
SR2	CM & St. P	125	95	65	
SR3	Along the CM & St. P	100	75	50	
SR4	Along the CM & St. P	125	95	65	
SR5	Along the CM & St. P	125	95	65	
SR6	Along the CM & St. P	85	65	45	
SR7	C & O, Safety First	350	250	175	
SR8	C & O	100	75	50	
SR9	C & O	100	75	50	
SR10	Denver & Rio Grande	50	40	25	
SR11	Denver & Rio Grande	350	250	175	
SR12	Denver & Salt Lake	200	150	100	
SR14	Great Northern Pacific SS	400	300	200	
SR15	Golden West, Lake	60	45	30	
SR16	Golden West, Mt. Shasta	60	45	30	
SR17	Southern Pacific	50	40	25	
SR18	Southern Pacific (Union Pacific)	350	250	175	
SR19	Southern Pacific	100	75	50	
SR20	Southern Pacific	20	15	10	
SR21	Southern Pacific	25	20	15	
SR22	Overland, Devil's Slide	150	115	75	
SR23	Union Pacific	50	40	25	
SR24	Western Pacific	40	30	20	
SR25	Rock Island	400	300	200	
		ALL PRICES IN U.S. DOLLARS			

REF. #	TITLE	MINT	EXCELLENT	VERY GOOD	NOTES
SR26	Rock Island	$ 500	$ 400	$ 250	
SR27	Seaboard Railway	250	200	125	
SR28	White Pass & Yukon	125	95	65	
SR29	White Pass & Yukon	125	95	65	
SR30	White Pass & Yukon	80	60	40	
SR31	White Pass & Yukon	80	60	40	
SR32	The Soo Line	1,500	1,100	800	
CANADIAN SCENIC • PAGES 269–272					
SCA 1	British Columbia	80	60	40	
SCA 2	British Columbia	80	60	40	
SCA 3	Atlantic to Great Lakes	75	60	40	
SCA 4	Atlantic to Great Lakes	200	150	100	
SCA 5	Atlantic to Great Lakes	250	190	125	
SCA 6	Grand Trunk	300	225	150	
SCA 7	Montreal & Quebec, CPCC	50	40	25	
SCA 8	Montreal & Quebec, Goodall	75	60	40	
SCA 9	Montreal & Quebec, Goodall	75	60	40	
SCA10	Montreal & Quebec, Goodall	75	60	40	
SCA11	King George V	90	70	50	
SCA12	King George V, plumed hat	200	150	100	
SCA13	Ocean to Ocean	75	60	40	
SCA14	Ocean to Ocean	60	45	30	
SCA15	Ocean to Ocean	50	40	25	
SCA16	Ocean to Ocean	80	60	40	
SCA17	Picturesque Canada, Goodall	100	75	50	
SCA18	Picturesque Canada, CPCC	350	275	175	
SCA19	Picturesque Canada, Goodall	200	150	100	
SCA20	Picturesque Canada, USPC	45	35	20	
SCA21	Picturesque Canada, CLL	75	60	40	
SCA22	Picturesque Canada, CLL	75	60	40	
SCA23	Picturesque Canada for CPR	200	150	100	
SCA24	Toronto	200	150	100	
SCA25	British Columbia	250	200	125	
SCA26	Manitoba	200	150	100	
SCA27	Ontario	200	150	100	
SCA28	Intercolonial RR	350	275	200	
SCA29	Intercolonial RR	300	225	150	
SCA30	Intercolonial RR	125	90	65	
SCA31	Winnipeg	300	225	150	
SCA32	Newfoundland	125	100	65	
SCA33	Ocean to Ocean	300	225	150	
SCU1	Cuba	65	50	35	
SCU2	Cuba, dancers	300	225	150	
SCU3	Cuba	125	100	65	
SO1	South Africa	125	100	65	
SO2	Tasmania	250	200	125	
SO3	Peru	250	200	125	
SO4	Peru	250	200	125	
		ALL PRICES IN U.S. DOLLARS			

REF. #	TITLE	MINT	EXCELLENT	VERY GOOD	NOTES
COLLEGES, UNIVERSITIES AND UNIONS • PAGES 273–276					
CU1	Yale, Marshall	$ 600	$ 450	$ 300	
CU1a	Harvard, Marshall	600	450	300	
CU2	Princeton, Marshall	550	425	275	
CU3	Ivy League, Yale	300	225	150	
CU3a	Ivy League, Harvard	250	200	125	
CU4	Congress Universities	250	200	125	
CU5	College Cards, c1920	60	45	30	
CU6	College, after 1930	20	15	10	
CU7	College Atheletes	20	15	10	
UN1	A. Eldon Duke	1,200	900	600	
UN2	Rexall Clubs	300	225	150	
UN3	National Lithographers	300	225	150	
UN4	Carpenters and Joiners	250	200	125	
UN4a	Other Early Wide Union	200	150	100	
UN5	International Pressman (O16)	350	275	175	
UN6	Amalgamated Meat Cutters	25	20	15	
BRIDGE/WHIST • PAGES 277–284					
BW1	Ames Whist Lessons	250	190	125	
BW2	Foster's Whist	100	75	50	
BW3	Foster Whist (2nd Series)	100	75	50	
BW4	Foster's Bridge	90	70	45	
BW5	Bird's Duplicate Whist	200	150	100	
BW6	Virginia Bridge	125	100	65	
BW6a	Virginia Skat	125	100	65	
BW7	Whist League, Dougherty	300	225	150	
BW8	Whist League, National	125	95	65	
BW8a	Whist League, American	200	150	100	
BW9	Work's Par Auction	50	40	25	
BW10	Work's Lessons in Auction	40	30	20	
BW11	Educator Bridge	50	40	25	
BW12	Point Count Dots, NYCC	50	40	25	
BW13	Gem #51 Point Count Dots	100	75	50	
BW14	Crest Approach Forcing	50	40	25	
BW15	Crest Official System	50	40	25	
BW16	Huntley Approach Forcing	110	85	55	
BW17	Huntley Official System	125	95	65	
BW18	Easibid, Fairchild	25	20	15	
BW19	Easibid, NYCC	50	40	25	
BW19a	Easibid, USPC	30	25	15	
BW20	Culbertson's Own	75	60	40	
BW21	Utility Deck	40	30	20	
BW22	James Bell, Newark	100	75	50	
BW23	Olympic, 1933	50	40	25	
BW24	Olympic, 1934	50	40	25	
BW25	Goren Bridgepoint	15	15	10	
BW26	Point Count, B&B	20	15	10	
		ALL PRICES IN U.S. DOLLARS			

REF. #	TITLE	MINT	EXCELLENT	VERY GOOD	NOTES
BW27	I-Deal	$ 100	$ 75	$ 50	
BW28	Bridge with Goren	20	15	10	
BW29	Rogers Auction Bridge	125	95	65	
BW30	Master Bridge	150	115	75	
BW31	Milton Work	50	40	25	
BW32	12 Tests, Bridge Headquarters	50	40	25	
BW33	Bridge Headquarters, USPC	25	20	15	
BW34	Varian Whist Cards	300	225	150	
BW35	Culbertson, Kem	35	30	20	
BW36	George Gooden	25	20	15	
BW37	Whist Instruction	300	225	150	
NO REVOKE • PAGES 285–288					
NR1	Seminole Wars (W2)	14,000	9,000	7,000	
NR2	Mauger Centennial (SX1)	2,400	1,800	1,200	
NR3	Sturbridge Repro	20	15	10	
NR4	Russell Regulars (W19)	350	265	175	
NR5	Petryl Green Spade, 53 cards	3,000	2,200	1,500	
NR6	Golden Diamond	100	75	50	
NR6a	Blue Spade	125	95	65	
NR6b	Green Club	75	60	40	
NR6c	Sweet Heart	750	500	300	
NR7	NU Fashion, Lefebure	100	75	50	
NR8	New Index	30	25	15	
NR9	Nuart	1,500	1,200	750	
NR9a	Nuart	800	600	400	
NR10	Ideal, Hurd	80	60	40	
NR11	Innovation, Criterion	80	60	40	
NR12	Huntley No-revoke	60	45	30	
NR13	Avoid	75	60	40	
NR14	Avoid 2	75	60	40	
NR15	EZ2C	60	45	30	
NR16	Forcolar	25	20	15	
NR17	Forcolar II	25	20	15	
NEW SUIT SIGNS • PAGES 289–293					
NS1	Union (W5)	1,000	750	500	
NS2	Union (W6)	1,600	1,200	800	
NS3	Army & Navy (W11)	6,000	4,500	3,000	
NS4	Bad Joker (P2)	4,000	3,000	2,000	
NS5	Dutton's (W18)	500	375	250	
NS6	Militac (W40)	80	60	40	
NS7	Military (W27)	40	30	20	
NS8	Roodles	50	40	25	
NS9	Prince Charles	750	600	375	
NS10	Bouquet	1,500	1,100	750	
NS11	Calendar	300	225	150	
NS12	Kon Quest	200	150	100	
NS13	ANMA (W35)	40	30	20	

ALL PRICES IN U.S. DOLLARS

REF. #	TITLE	MINT	EXCELLENT	VERY GOOD	NOTES
NS14	Jan Ken Po	$ 100	$ 75	$ 50	
NS15	Rumme	75	60	40	
NS16	Hiram Jones 6 Suit	375	300	200	
NS17	Secobra 6 Suit	40	30	20	
NS18	Eagle 5 Suit, USPC	30	25	15	
NS19	Eagle 5 Suit, Russell	30	25	15	
NS20	Castle 5 Suit	50	40	25	
NS21	Arrco 5 Suit	40	30	20	
NS22	Crompton 5 Suit	100	75	50	
NS23	Court of Music	500	350	250	
NS24	America	500	375	250	
NS25	Philitis	750	550	350	
NS26	Hand 'em a Lemon	75	60	40	
NS27	Pahlavi	375	300	200	
ODDITIES • PAGES 295–299					
O1	Pan-Am Aluminum (SX19)	800	600	400	
O2	St. Louis Aluminum (SX20)	1,000	750	500	
O3	King Aluminum	300	225	150	
O4	Celluloid Co.	250	200	125	
O4a	Piroxloid Co.	250	200	125	
O5	Celluloid, Whitehead & Hoag	450	325	225	
O5a	Celluloid, Whitehead & Hoag	350	275	175	
O6	Asbestos	150	115	75	
O7	Kling Magnetic	15	15	10	
O8	Magna Cards	25	20	15	
O9	Clark's Tiles	80	60	40	
O10	Dur-o-Deck Tiles	70	55	35	
O11	I.N. Richardson	200	150	100	
O11a	I.N. Richardson	200	150	100	
O12	I.W. Richardson	200	150	100	
O13	Globe, Cornhill	300	225	150	
O14	Globe, Hawley	250	190	125	
O15	Waterproof	250	190	150	
O16	International	250	190	150	
O17	Sutherland Coon Cards	350	225	150	
O18	Discus	25	20	15	
O19	Arrco	15	15	10	
O20	Transparent, Nelson	2,500	2,000	1,250	
O20a	Transparent, Michauds	1,500	1,100	750	
O20b	Transparent	1,500	1,100	750	
O20c	Transparent	1,200	900	600	
O21	Transparent PCC	1,500	1,150	750	
O22	Transparent, American	1,500	1,150	750	
O23	Transparent	1,500	1,150	750	
O24	New Era Concave	35	30	20	
O25	EZ Rectangular	30	25	15	
O26	Crooked Deck	15	15	10	
		ALL PRICES IN U.S. DOLLARS			

REF. #	TITLE	MINT	EXCELLENT	VERY GOOD	NOTES
O27	Contoura	$ 35	$ 30	$ 20	
O28	Globe, Miller & Montgomery	350	275	200	
O29	Globe, Globe PCC	350	275	200	
O30	Buffard Transparent	1,500	1,200	750	
O31	Grandmother Stover	25	20	15	
O32	DeLand Tiny	300	225	150	
NOVELTY • PAGES 301–309					
N1	Put & Take	150	115	75	
N2	DeLand's Automatic, Adams	50	40	25	
N2a	DeLand's Automatic, Deland	250	200	125	
N3	DeLand's Nifty, Adams	50	40	25	
N3a	DeLand's Nifty	450	325	250	
N4	DeLand's Daisy, Adams	50	40	25	
N5	DeLand's Star, Adams	50	40	25	
N6	Adam's League	50	40	25	
N7	Super	50	40	25	
N8	Buster Brown	125	90	60	
N9	Teddy Bear	400	300	200	
N10	Boob Deck	140	110	70	
N11	Carnival	200	150	100	
N12	Mardi Gras	400	300	200	
N13	Pepper	250	190	125	
N14	Double Action	50	40	25	
N14a	Double Action, Stancraft	40	30	20	
N15	Duplex Deck	100	75	50	
N16	Chess	300	225	150	
N17	Dice	200	150	100	
N18	Vanity	400	300	200	
N19	Hycrest Royalty	500	400	250	
N20	Inca	50	40	25	
N21	Maya	50	40	25	
N22	Photo	100	75	50	
N23	Bannister Babies (P7)	35	30	20	
N24	Bannister Babies 2	35	30	20	
N25	Monkey Capers	35	30	20	
N26	Believe It or Not	40	30	20	
N27	Tee Up	20	15	10	
N28	Fish Up	20	15	10	
N29	Bowl Up	20	15	10	
N30	Cheer Up	20	15	10	
N31	Drink Up	20	15	10	
N32	Tune Up	20	15	10	
N33	Stag Party	30	25	15	
N33a	Stag Party	30	25	15	
N33b	Stag Party	30	25	15	
N34	Peppy	30	25	15	
N35	Vargas Vanities	90	70	50	
		ALL PRICES IN U.S. DOLLARS			

REF. #	TITLE	MINT	EXCELLENT	VERY GOOD	NOTES
N36	Art Ball	$ 50	$ 40	$ 25	
N37	Museum of Modern Art	50	40	25	
N38	Eska Calorie	20	15	10	
N39	Trip Trap	55	45	30	
N40	Royal Flash	50	40	25	
N41	Survival	40	30	20	
N42	Green Cross	20	15	10	
N43	O-Shlemiel	20	15	10	
N44	Sheba	20	15	10	
N45	Soul Cards	25	20	15	
N46	Fact & Fancy	50	40	25	
N47	Mythological Zoo, hand-colored	90	70	45	
N48	Love Scenes	2,000	1,500	1,000	
N48a	War Scenes	2,500	1,850	1,250	
N49	Check Your Catch	50	40	25	
N50	Authors, Singer	300	225	150	
N51	Cudahy, Bar S	40	30	20	
N52	McLoughlin	150	115	75	
N53	Imperial Automobile	300	225	150	
N54	Telbax	200	150	100	
N55	Midget	100	75	50	
		ALL PRICES IN U.S. DOLLARS			

Front of U.S. & National Playing Cards Price List, circa 1890.

NOTES

NOTES

NOTES

The Elks.

Knights of Pythias.

No. 888.

Mystic

Playing Cards.

Secret Society Designs.

Emblematic Backs and Jokers.

Goat Back—for general use.

Linen Stock.

Telescope Cases.

Clear-cut, conventional faces.

Sold by dealers.

Sample pack,
Plain edges, . 50c.
Gold edges, . 60c.

Copyrighted, 1898, by

The United States Playing Card Company

CINCINNATI, U. S. A.

Odd-Fellows.

Shriner.